SHIPWRECK

Tales of Survival, Courage & Calamity at Sea

Louise Callan

Hodder Moa Beckett

Author's Acknowledgements

Shipwreck the book owes its life to *Shipwreck* the television series, produced by Greenstone Pictures for Television New Zealand's TV One. It was the production team from Greenstone who undertook the initial research and chose, from the hundreds of shipwrecks that litter New Zealand's coastal waters, the 11 wrecks whose stories are told here. And it was the intensive sleuthing of the programme's researchers – Denene Marten, Peter Bell, Trevor Conn, Vivienne Jeffs, Jane Reeves and Mark Derby – through old records, newspapers, diaries and letters, and their tracing of descendants and survivors, that provided the rich detail necessary to retell the stories in book form.

Thanks, too, to the series producer, Tony Manson, for leaving me to tell the stories for the book the way I thought best; and to Carmel Williams and Rachel Antony, my constant links to Greenstone, for providing whatever additional help was needed, whenever it was needed.

Along with Greenstone Pictures' research, I was also extremely lucky to inherit the careful eye and extensive nautical and historical knowledge of Gavin McLean, senior historian at the Historical Branch of Internal Affairs. Thanks are due him for his time, expertise and suggestions; and to his colleague Angela Ballara from the *Dictionary of New Zealand Biography*.

Karen Holdom is owed special thanks for her major contribution to the book – she wrote the chapters on the two Second World War wrecks: the *Niagara* and the *Turakina*. Karen evokes all the drama, emotion and heroism of their sinking in a period of growing national tension.

Many of the fascinating old images in the book were made available by Rosemary Tarlton of Kelly Tarlton's Shipwreck Museum, Waitangi, Bay of Islands.

Finally, I want to thank the editorial team at Hodder Moa Beckett for their generous support, enthusiasm and professionalism: Janette Howe, managing editor; Graham Adams, copy editor; Maria McGivern, editorial assistant; and Nick Turzynski, art director.

Every endeavour has been made to trace and contact the owners of photographic copyright. This was not possible in some cases and the publisher apologises for any inadvertent omissions.

ISBN 1-86958-784-7

© 2000 – Original text – Greenstone Pictures
The moral rights of the author have been asserted

© 2000 Design and format – Hodder Moa Beckett Publishers Limited

Published under licence from TVNZ Enterprises

Published in 2000 by Hodder Moa Beckett Publishers Limited, [a member of the Hodder Headline Group] 4 Whetu Place, Mairangi Bay, Auckland, New Zealand

Produced and designed by Hodder Moa Beckett Publishers Ltd

Film by Microdot, Auckland
Printed by South China Printing, Hong Kong

All rights reserved. No part of this publication may be reproduced or transmitted in any form or by any means, electronic or mechanical, including photocopying, recording, or any information storage and retrieval system, without permission in writing from the publisher.

Contents

introduction	4	Adrift – The Lost Survivors of the ELiNGAMiTE	80
The Tragedy of the BOYD	6	Dead Reckoning – The Wreck of the WiLTSHiRE	92
The Wreck of the ORPHEUS	18	The Treasure of the NiAGARA	104
The Wreck of the DELAWARE – Huria's Story	30	The Battle of the TURAKiNA	116
The TARARUA Tragedy	42	The Mystery of the HOLMGLEN	128
Black Sunday – The Wreck of the BEN VENUE	56	Glossary	142
The ARiADNE Agreement	68	References	144

Simon Young

"There lies the port; the vessel puffs her sail: There gloom the dark broad seas."
Alfred Lord Tennyson, "Ulysses"

I write this introduction not as a specialist of maritime history but as a professional storyteller. Television is all about telling stories and there is something about a ship breaking up on a reef or foundering in a hurricane that immediately captures the imagination and stirs the emotions.

All the stories in this book are true, which for me makes them even more compelling. They are stories of unimaginable hardship and disappointment, incredible triumphs, tragic personal loss and daring rescue.

I understand there have been over 2000 shipwrecks on New Zealand's often treacherous coastline. Some are unremarkable, but many are gripping tales of calamity and heroism. This rich history gave us our first research challenge: which stories to leave out of the television series?

Many meetings and cups of coffee later our small research team narrowed down the material to the vivid stories included in the following pages: 11 shipwreck sagas, beginning with the grim and bloody tale of the *Boyd* in 1809 and ending with the

INTRODUCTION

mystery of the disappearance of the *Holmglen* and her crew in 1959.

Against an epic backdrop of towering waves and hurricane gales these shipwrecks not only sample 150 years of our maritime history but also recount the personal tales of New Zealand settlers, travellers, fortune seekers, sailors, immigrants and traders – people whose lives were changed forever by one moment of peril at sea.

I thank New Zealand On Air and TVNZ for funding the *Shipwreck* series – allowing us to tell New Zealand stories to fellow New Zealanders.

I want to thank Paul Gittins for his commitment to the storytelling process and for enduring the discomfort of many days filming at sea and on rocky, remote coastlines. My thanks also to the story directors, the production team, and the crew. Their work was not simply a creative challenge – how to make a placid sea look like a storm, a piece of hardboard pass for the hull of a ship – but a test of stamina. On the road for 12 weeks, the crew travelled the length and breadth of the country with nearly 400 kilograms of television equipment in tow.

I thank Dr Gavin McLean for his specialist historical advice; Wade Doak and Keith Gordon for generously offering their nautical expertise. I also owe a debt of gratitude to the research team – Denene Marten, Peter Bell, Trevor Conn, Vivienne Jeffs, Jane Reeves and Mark Derby – who sifted through the archives and libraries for yellowing newspaper reports, personal letters, diaries, maritime inquiries, photographs and old film footage.

My thanks also to all those descendants who contributed family memories, photographs and personal records.

Also of great help with our research and filming were a number of libraries, museums, archives and newspapers throughout the country. The New Zealand National Maritime Museum, the Whangaroa Museum (Kaeo), the Alexander Turnbull Library (National Library of New Zealand – Te Puna Matauranga o Aotearoa), the Museum of New Zealand – Te Papa Tongarewa, NZTV Archive, Huia Settlers Museum Incorporated, Auckland City Libraries, Auckland Museum – Te Papa Whakahiku, Natural History New Zealand, North Otago Museum (Oamaru), Museum of Wellington City and Sea, Canterbury Museum, Hocken Library (University of Otago), Waikawa Museum, Wyndham and Districts Historical Society, *New Zealand Herald*, *Timaru Herald*, South Canterbury Museum, Sound Archives (Nga Taonga Korero), all contributed significantly to our production.

Finally, special thanks to writer Louise Callan for turning pictures back into words again and offering us such a graphic record of these moments of adventure from our New Zealand past. I'm sure these stories will find a place on the bookshelves of many New Zealand homes and baches.

Tony Manson
Producer: *Shipwreck*

Director Roz Mason with actors during filming of the story, "Dead Reckoning – The Wreck of the *Wiltshire*".

Simon Young

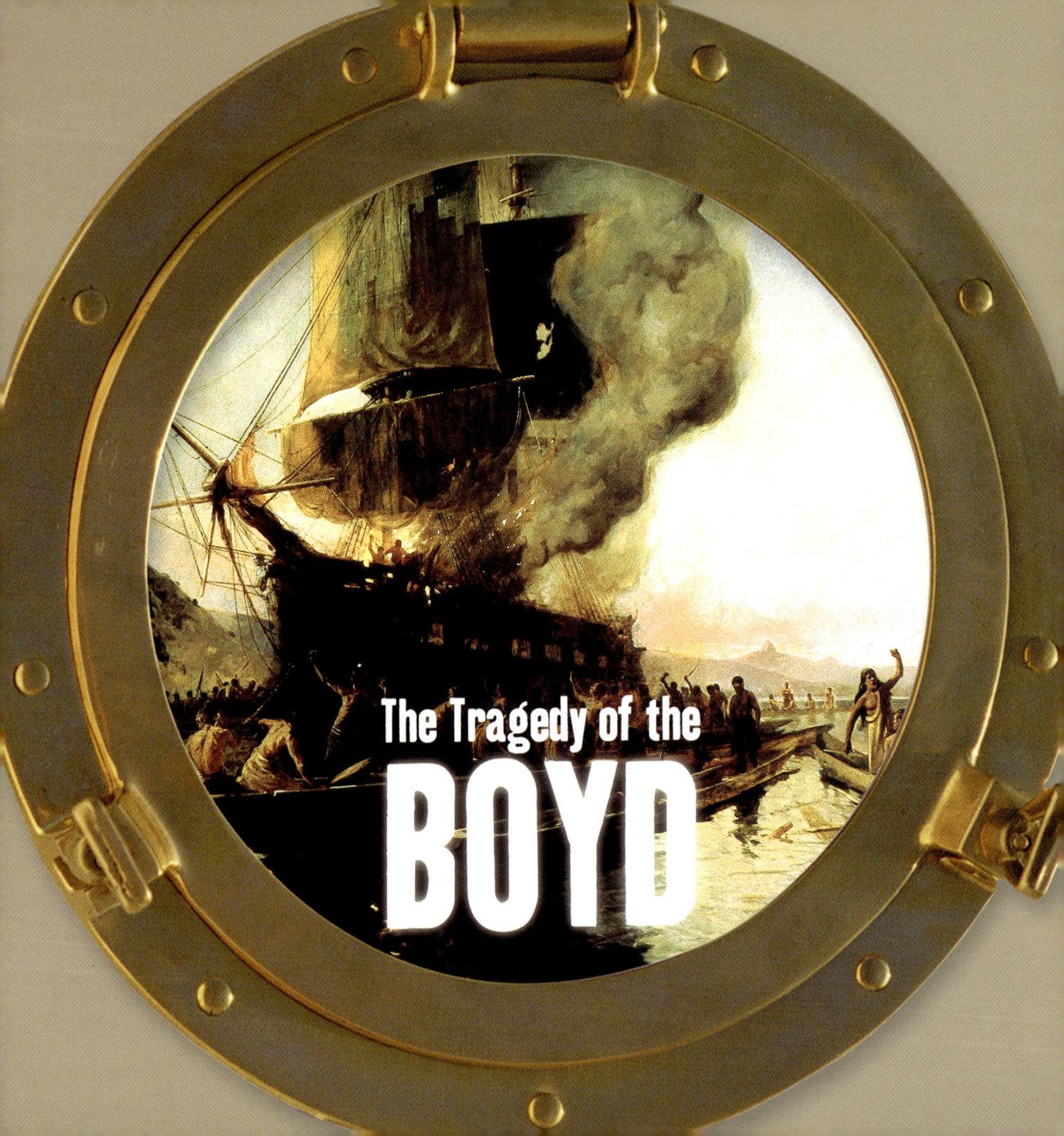

The Tragedy of the BOYD

The social and political currents and forces which drove the *Boyd* to its destruction were as relentless and powerful as the forces of nature that drive vessels on to rocks or destroy them at sea. At the beginning of the 1800s, a scant 30 years had passed since the Maori's first substantive contact with the outside world, through Captain Cook and the crew of *Endeavour*.

The Boyd

Type: brigantine
Tonnage: 392 tons
Owner: George Brown, London
Master: Captain John Thompson
Crew and passengers: 75 approximately
Cargo: NSW mahogany, seal skins, oil and coal valued at £15,000
Destined voyage: Port Jackson, Sydney—London
Date of departure: November 1809
Date of wreck: December 1809
Location of wreck: Whangaroa, Bay of Islands
Lives lost: 66 approximately

The story of the *Boyd* was set within the emerging struggle between chiefs of the Bay of Islands region for the patronage of the European; and competition to provide goods and services to the visiting ships in exchange for iron — nails, fish hooks and metal tools — the first New Zealand "currency".

Captain Philip Gidley King of the Royal Navy, Governor of both Norfolk Island and New South Wales, had a fascination with Maori and dreamt of becoming Governor of New Zealand. After King visited New Zealand bringing gifts of pigs, seed potatoes and tools, Bay of Islands chief Te Pahi and his four sons travelled to Port Jackson, Sydney, in 1805 to meet him. From the outset, both men made plain that they saw benefits in establishing a relationship. King wrote that "the kindness this family received at our hand would be abundantly repaid to the English whalers frequenting the Bay of Islands".[1]

Te Pahi made the most of his three-month stay in Sydney. He was curious about almost every aspect of life in the colony, especially practical skills such as horticulture, carpentry, spinning and weaving. The Reverend Samuel Marsden recorded, "He possessed a clear, strong, and comprehensive mind, and was anxious to gain what knowledge he could of our laws and customs. He was wont to converse much with me about our God, and was very regular in his attendance at church on the Sabbath; and when at public worship behaved with great decorum."[2] The *Sydney Gazette* described him as a friendly chief "about fifty years of age; 5 feet 11 and a half inches high and of an athletic form: His countenance is expressive and commanding, though much disfigured by his face being completely tattowed [sic]".[3] King recognised his chiefly status and described him as "stout and extremely well made…. To say that he was nearly civilized falls far short of his character, as every action and observation shows an

SHIPWRECK

uncommon attention to the rules of decency and propriety in his every action, and has much of the airs and manners of a man conversant in the world he lives in."[4]

Te Pahi returned home laden with gifts from King and other citizens of Sydney. When the ship left his island settlement Te Puna to return to Port Jackson, it carried gifts for King and Te Pahi's friends in Sydney – seven spars for ships' masts, flax and flax cloth, fishing lines, weapons, and good seed potatoes. A very public relationship had been established. The chief's voyage home also brought about a more personal alliance. During the four-week trip, Te Pahi became very ill and was nursed by a young man called George Bruce (in the ship's log his name is "Joseph Druce"). He had just been given a pardon by Governor King after spending several years on the run to avoid a sentence of 200 lashes for his part in a pub brawl. But on board he got into trouble again. While the vessel was anchored at an island off North Cape, trading with locals there and exploring, "Joseph Druce was flogged for 'theft, disobedience and embezzlement'". Just before they sailed on for the Bay of Islands, or after they reached there, Bruce jumped ship. A few months later, he turned up at Te Puna where he was married to Te Pahi's youngest daughter, Atahoe.

While George Bruce was being initiated into the ways of the Maori and tattooed as a warrior, Te Pahi was introducing his people to some European practices. His potato gardens expanded and he planted maize for the first time. He also introduced whipping as a punishment for theft. He had talked to King about sending some of his people to Sydney to learn spinning, weaving and carpentry, and dispatched his son Matara on another voyage, this time to England. Te Pahi's admiration of European things continued, despite what he was experiencing on his home territory. He told Governor King that "he would never be able to restrain his countrymen from inflicting cruel outrages upon Europeans unless the Governor would put a stop to the practice roving sea captains had adopted of flogging Maori chiefs, as that was an indignity no Maori chief would ever lose an opportunity to revenge".[5] King had issued a public warning against such practices. A sworn statement to Marsden on the cruel and violent way in which the generosity of the local tribes was repaid stated:

"I have no doubt but that the Natives would be kind and attentive to the Crews of the Ships that put in there, if they were treated with any degree of common Justice honesty and civility."[6]

The new Governor of New South Wales, Captain William Bligh, responded to these complaints by forbidding ships from taking local people from the islands of the Pacific to Britain. Later that year, 1807, Captain David Dalrymple's vessel, the *General Wellesley*, arrived in the Bay of Islands carrying a few passengers and looking for timber. George Bruce organised Te Pahi's people to cut and load spars. The ship's crew had already had an unnecessarily violent confrontation with the islanders of the Tuamotus. After their

Te Pahi

Te Pahi was one of the senior chiefs in the western Bay of Islands, a descendant of Ngati Awa and their conquerors Nga Puhi, and related to Ngati Rehia and probably to Te Hikutu and Ngati Rua.

Auckland City Art Gallery

"The burning of the *Boyd*"

Walter Wright painted the best-known picture of the *Boyd* in 1908 almost a hundred years after its destruction. It is a far from accurate illustration of what took place, but suited the European sentiments of the time: that most Maori were savages with few redeeming features and their disappearance as a race inevitable. Politics and social attitudes have played a part in the story of the *Boyd* right from the beginning.

Te Puhi

Te Ara and Te Puhi (Te Pahi's father-in-law) of Ngati Uru, one of the two hapu banished from the Bay of Islands after killing French explorer Marion du Fresne in 1772, played a part in the loss of the *Boyd*.

Te Ara

arrival in New Zealand waters, there was another incident when local war canoes tried to trap a boat from the *General Wellesley* near where Marion du Fresne was killed. Dalrymple then asked Bruce to accompany him while he sailed to North Cape to look for "gold dust" said to be there. On the way north, they called in to Whangaroa Harbour and picked up his wife, Atahoe, and three young Maori sailors. But, as with so much of Bruce's life, events were against him. The gold was fool's gold and before he, Atahoe and the others could leave the ship, a storm drove it out to sea. Dalrymple then continued his voyage to India, with the desperate New Zealanders still on board. Relations deteriorated. They were thrown out of their cabin and made to work. Another passenger blamed their situation on Bruce's abusive behaviour. When the ship docked in Malacca, the captain sold one of the young Maori as a slave and sailed away while George Bruce was still on shore. In Penang, Dalrymple sold Atahoe into slavery as a lady's maid.

During 1808, the level of violence and ill will between Maori and European whalers and traders increased. When the *Parramatta* arrived at the Bay of Islands drastically low in supplies, local iwi provided food and water. But when they asked for payment they were thrown overboard, fired at and wounded. The *Parramatta* sailed off only to be driven ashore again during a storm. Retribution followed – the ship was plundered and the crew killed, but its fate was not discovered until three years later. Until then it was believed lost at sea.

Te Pahi and his people suffered in the deteriorating conditions. Food stores and gardens were raided repeatedly by sailors, the locals beaten and their belongings stolen. Then, during a visit to a vessel where his people had arranged to exchange 20 baskets of potatoes for 20 nails, Te Pahi was accused of trying to cheat them in providing only 19 baskets. The furious captain tied him to the rigging in pouring rain. It was five or six hours before he was freed, and only after another basket was delivered, "tho' Tippahee offered to go on shore in his own Canoe… and bring him the Potatoes".[7] Later it was discovered one of the sailors had stolen the potatoes. It was "a terrible assault upon the mana of a chief, and Te Pahi and his people must have been extremely angry."[8]

By May 1808, Te Pahi could no longer endure the situation. With his sons he sailed again for Port Jackson to report the kidnapping of his daughter and son-in-law to Governor Bligh and complain once again about the Europeans' behaviour. The trip with Captain James Ceroni was ill fated from its beginning. As there was little food in the Bay, Te Pahi directed Ceroni to Whangaroa for supplies. Although this harbour was less than 50 kilometres to the north-east of the Bay of Islands, it remained unknown to Europeans until 1805, and the *Commerce* was only the third sailing ship to enter there.

> "Ceroni had a watch that he often showed to local people who thought it was an atua (or perhaps a waka atua – 'god receptacle'). To their horror, during one of these demonstrations Ceroni dropped the watch into Whangaroa Harbour. The *Commerce* sailed away that night without the usual farewells, and soon after she had sailed an epidemic broke out, killing many people, including the chief Kaitoke."[9]

During the voyage, Te Pahi himself became ill and by the time they arrived in Port Jackson he was very sick. In Sydney, he discovered that the man he had come to ask for help, Governor Bligh, was under house arrest after a mutiny by the military. He stayed with Bligh, watching a very different side to European power politics; but as soon as he was well, he was asked to leave Government House. Many of the people who had opened their homes to him when he was Governor King's guest now ignored him. He left without any promise of help with the mounting lawlessness back in the Bay of Islands.

Three weeks later, his son Matara arrived in Sydney after a successful visit to England. Alexander Berry, once a surgeon and now an influential merchant in Sydney, was asked by Governor Bligh to take Matara back to New Zealand, as Berry was on his way to the Bay to look for timber. Te Pahi and Berry had already met in Norfolk Island when Te Pahi and his sons stopped there on their second trip to Sydney. Berry's impressions of Te Pahi were scathing: "He was wearing certain robes of state presented to him by Governor King on his first visit. They were covered in tinsel and resembled to some extent those worn by a merry Andrew…. He… showed an easy consciousness of his own dignity… but the most prominent features of his character were a certain shrewdness and low cunning… much inferior to his countrymen of equal standing."[10]

Berry and Matara arrived in the Bay of Islands on 1 March 1809 on the *City of Edinburgh*. There was no spar timber to be had on the Te Puna side of the Bay. Te Pahi now urged Berry and his captain, Pattison, to cut timber on the land he had recently inherited on the death of chief Kaitoke, a victim of the disease which had ravaged Whangaroa after Ceroni's departure. It seems Berry and Pattison were looking for somewhere closer. They were told there was spar timber in the next district under the control of a chief called Tupi. Tupi was one of two Ngati Manu chiefs who controlled Kororareka and the Kawakawa district. They were part of a rival tribal alliance to Te Pahi and his allies.

Berry had a higher regard for the Kororareka chiefs than he had for Te Pahi. The older of the brothers, Tara, was then about 60 years old. According to Berry: "His general integrity might be depended on, and his word was sacred."[11] Tupi was much younger, spoke in a mixture of Maori and English and dressed in a motley of European clothes. Berry described him as having a "face and manner [that] equally bespoke a man of judgement and humanity". Tupi piloted the *City of Edinburgh* into the harbour at Kororareka and then, while Berry was making major repairs to his ship, warned him that his vessel was going to be attacked and captured. Berry did not believe him. But the following morning a number of war canoes arrived in the bay. They were driven off, many of the warriors killed and several canoes captured. One of the locals told Berry he had defeated the chief of Waitangi, one of Te Pahi's allies; and a few days later Matara appeared to ask him to return a couple of his father's canoes. He claimed that they had been stolen by "the bad people". Berry did not believe him, "but felt sorry to see him so much altered by illness. He spoke with hoarseness from congestion of the lungs. I gave him back the canoes…."[12]

Berry was ready to continue his passage through the Pacific in late May. The two

The Tragedy of
THE BOYD

National Library of Australia 14711

Governor Philip Gidley King

Governor King was one of the main players in the story of the *Boyd*, initiating contact between two very different worlds, hoping to bridge the cultural divide. There are always risks in such exchanges.

Alexander Berry

Berry was a Sydney merchant and trader and one of the settler oligarchy whose dislike and distrust of Te Pahi had fatal consequences. He believed that natives, like convicts, were irredeemable barbarians.

chiefs went with him to the harbour entrance. But before they reached the heads, Captain Ceroni, who was travelling with Berry, took out his watch to show the Maori and, incredibly, dropped this one over the side as well. "Tara now wrung his hands and wept in distress. 'Ceroni will be the destruction of the Bay of Islands, as he was at Whangaroa.' Tupe [sic] tried vainly to convince his brother not to be a fool, that a watch was not a demon…."[13] What Tupi did not tell Berry was that "death as the result of makutu or whaiwhaia (witchcraft) demanded retribution".[14]

By the end of October Berry was back, still looking for timber. He had set course for Whangaroa despite the tears and entreaties of the Maori sailors on board who told him the people there intended to attack the next ship to enter the harbour, in revenge for the epidemic and the death of their paramount chief, Kaitoke. However, the winds were against him and he sailed on to Kororareka, where Tara and Tupi welcomed him again.

When the *City of Edinburgh* had finished loading spars, Tara urged Berry to leave as soon as possible. He had been told the people of Whangaroa had captured a European ship, seized the guns and gunpowder, and killed and eaten the crew. Now they intended to come south to attack him. Once again, Berry didn't believe the chiefs. But as days passed, the rumours became more persistent. Finally, towards the end of December 1809, Berry decided to check the stories for himself. He asked for volunteers from his crew and three armed boats set out for Whangaroa. When he reached the deep sheltered harbour on the east coast of the Bay of Islands, he discovered the rumours were true.

"We found the wreck in shoal water at the top of the harbour, a most melancholy picture of wanton mischief. The natives had cut her cables and towed her up the harbour till she had grounded, and then set her on fire and burned her to the water's edge. In her hold were seen the remains of her cargo – coals, salted seal skins and planks. Her guns, iron standards, etc., were lying on the top, having fallen in when her decks were consumed.

"Metenangha [Matengaro] landed by himself but directed the boats to a more convenient landing place where he quickly joined us with two of the principal chiefs [probably Te Ara and Te Puhi] and several of their friends who had been engaged in the massacre. Dressed in canvas, the spoil of the ship, they approached us with the greatest confidence, held out their hands, and addressed me by name in the style and manner of old acquaintance."[15]

The charred and sunken wreck was all that remained of the brig *Boyd*, en route from Port Jackson to London. Berry asked whether there were any survivors and the men "answered readily in the affirmative, mentioning their names with great familiarity and even with the appearance of kindness and sympathy".[16] Berry gave them a choice: they could trade their captives for axes or he and his men would attack and take them by force. The chiefs hesitated briefly. Trading they said was better than fighting. Only five people had survived the massacre – a woman, Anne Morley, and her baby; a little girl, Betsey Broughton; and two members of the crew – a young boy, Thomas Davis, and the second mate. However, the mate was no longer alive. He had been given as a gift to another chief who wanted him to make fish hooks out of iron hoops but, Berry was told, "as he did not prove himself a good workman [the chief] killed and ate him".

Berry took the survivors and some of the chiefs from Whangaroa and returned to his ship where the Maori were put in irons. They would be released when all the books and papers from the *Boyd* were handed over. But once these were delivered, he changed his mind. He gathered the crew and all the Maori on board and told them they were to witness an execution.

> "I then address the chiefs, telling them that if an Englishman committed a single murder he was hanged; that they had massacred a whole ship's crew, and therefore could expect no mercy; but as they were chiefs I would not degrade them by hanging, but would shoot them. All on board except Metenangha [Matengaro] and the chiefs themselves were delighted. Old Tara seated himself before the mast…. Every time I passed he looked at me with his one eye, which was twinkling with pleasure, and he nodded his token of approval."[17]

According to Berry, Tara's son had been murdered by these chiefs during a friendly visit to Whangaroa. Berry loaded two muskets and asked two "South Sea Islanders" to act as executioners, firing only when he told them to.

"The chiefs looked stedfastly [sic] at the presented muskets and then covered up their faces with their mats in the same way Caesar did, that they might die with more decency. Some time elapsed before I gave the signal, and both chiefs at the same moment uncovered their faces to see what was the matter. The signal was now given; both fired at the same instant. The chiefs remained motionless, and everyone thought that they had expired without a groan."[18] In fact, Berry had carefully loaded the guns with powder but no shot. He told them rather than death their punishment was the degradation of becoming slaves of the people of Kororareka. Tara was particularly pleased, promising lasting friendship with "the Pakeha or Whiteman".

A few days later in early January, the *City of Edinburgh* sailed for Valparaiso and Lima with the survivors. But before they left, Berry and Pattison wrote an account of what had happened to be issued as a warning for other ships visiting the region. He left a copy with Tara to show to all visiting captains. In the Notice, Berry stated that "this shocking event… according to the most satisfactory information was perpetrated entirely under the direction of that old rascal Te Pahi who had been so much and so undeservedly caressed at Port Jackson".[19] He said that after the ship's captain and some of his men had been led into the bush to look for suitable timber for spars, Te Pahi gave a signal and the many Maori on board the *Boyd* threw aside their cloaks to reveal weapons. They attacked and killed all those on board except for a few who escaped

Elizabeth Isabella Broughton

This portrait of Betsey Broughton was commissioned by her father after her eventual return to NSW. He sent it as a gift to the family in Lima, Peru, who cared for her for almost a year.

into the rigging. Te Pahi convinced them it was safe to come down and then watched as they were slaughtered. The captain and crew had been killed in the bush.

Berry concluded the Notice with a warning: "let no man after this trust a New Zealander." The sources of his "satisfactory information" were probably Matengaro, who went with him to Whangaroa and claimed a connection with the Whangaroa hapu, and Te Ara. The latter was no friend of Te Pahi and his allies and both men would have used Te Pahi's presence as a useful way to deflect retribution from their people.[20] Before the *City of Edinburgh* sailed, Berry also dispatched a letter to the new Governor of New South Wales, Lachlan Macquarie, once again blaming Te Pahi for the loss of the ship and slaughter of its crew and passengers.

News of the massacre and burning of the *Boyd* and the accusations against Te Pahi reached Port Jackson in March 1810, only days after the *Sydney Gazette* announced the death of the chief's daughter, Atahoe. Her husband, George Bruce, had managed to trace and rescue her from the naval captain who had bought her for his wife. During their return voyage, Atahoe gave birth to a daughter. In Sydney, Atahoe became sick with dysentery and died. Bruce had been hired by a group of traders to lead an expedition to New Zealand to set up a flax settlement. But within days of his wife's death and the announcement of his father-in-law's role in the attack on the *Boyd*, his contract was cancelled. Once again he was in danger of arrest for desertion. He abandoned his daughter in the Female Orphan School and escaped to England.

As news of the *Boyd* spread from Sydney to Calcutta, Paris and London, Te Pahi's name quickly became synonymous with the "ignoble savage". He was accused of treachery and painted as a violent, bloodthirsty monster who had tricked men like King and the missionary Samuel Marsden into trusting and admiring him. But not everyone believed Berry's account of the events. Marsden and some others claimed Te Pahi was "innocent and noble, a victim of brutal degraded Europeans".[21] Marsden, in particular, did not believe Te Pahi was guilty and spent a number of years searching for witnesses and information that would clear his name.

Five months after the first news of the loss of the *Boyd* reached Sydney, a revised account of what had happened was published in the *Sydney Gazette*, spread over two issues in September 1810. This second story came from the same source as the first, the American whaler Captain Chace of the *King George*, who had brought back Berry's version. This time Chace had talked to a Tahitian called Tom who had sailed with the *City of Edinburgh* and had left the vessel while it was moored in the Bay of Islands. He had been living ashore when the *Boyd* was attacked. The *Gazette* finished its new report with the comment that this was the most probable account of what had happened "the more especially so as it is the report of an Otaihetan, who was on the spot at the time, and who, as an alien, may still more be entitled to credit".[22]

The *Boyd*, captained by John Thompson, had called at the Bay of Islands to top up its hold with kauri spars. It had a cargo of timber, seal skins, coal and oil valued at £15,000. There were about 70 Europeans on board, crew and passengers, and four or five Maori. Among the latter was a Ngati Uru chief from Whangaroa, Te Ara, or

George as he was known to Europeans, who had sailed on several sealing expeditions.

Te Ara and the others were probably the first Maori Captain Thompson had met, and with no previous knowledge of Maori customs and culture, or their country, their attempts to adopt European clothing and manners and the rough English learnt at sea no doubt made them seem presumptuous and uncouth. Te Ara had been described in very unflattering terms by a missionary who met him in Sydney: "His features were not unsightly, but they appeared to veil a dark and subtle malignity of intention…. He had acquired, too, from his intercourses with European sailors, a coarse familiarity of manner, mingled with a degree of sneering impudence, which gave him a character completely distinct from his countrymen."[23] Some Maori claimed later the *Boyd* and its passengers had been attacked because of the deadly spell cast by Ceroni when he dropped his watch in the harbour and the many deaths from the sickness that followed. But many others said it was the direct result of the way Te Ara was treated during the Tasman crossing.

There is disagreement about what exactly took place on the voyage but it is generally agreed that Captain Thompson treated Te Ara harshly. Discipline aboard ship was hard, conditions often terrible and pay no more than a pittance. The Maori were to work their passage and if Thompson treated them any differently, the rest of the crew would regard him as weak. In a letter to Governor Brisbane in 1823, Te Ara said Thompson had him flogged three times. He told the missionary Nicholas that "he was taken so ill during the voyage as to be utterly incapable of doing his duty, which the captain not believing, and imputing his inability to work rather to laziness than indisposition, he was threatened, insulted, and abused by him, and tied up to the gangway and flogged most severely".[24] When he protested that he was a chief and should not be "degraded by punishment" the captain replied that he was only a slave, adding insult to injury.

Te Ara knew the captain wanted spars to complete his cargo and, concealing his anger, invited him to Whangaroa. Once they had anchored, the chief went ashore and told his tribe what had happened. He showed them the marks of the flogging on his back. The massacre of the captain and crew was planned as utu for the great insult done to the chief and his people.

Three days after their arrival, Thompson and three armed boatloads of his men were taken into the bush to inspect trees for spars. Once there, Te Ara attacked Thompson and killed him. The rest of the Maori attacked the other sailors with clubs and axes, killed them and later ate them. They stripped the sailors and dressed in their clothes, then took the boats back out to the ship that night and told the second mate that Thompson had decided to sleep on shore. They were to start loading spars but when they got on board, they began killing the remaining crew and the passengers. Four or five men managed to escape and climb into the rigging. Anne Morley and the two children hid below, while the cabin boy Thomas Davis pleaded with Te Ara for his life. Davis said later the chief had let him live saying he was "a good boy", but another Maori claimed it was his club foot that saved him – it was taken as a sign of supernatural power.

Te Pahi arrived next morning, apparently to trade fish, and was extremely angry when he discovered what had happened. He told the men still in the rigging he would

William Broughton, Deputy Commissary General

William Broughton came to Australia as a servant on the First Fleet. His common law wife, ex-convict Elizabeth Heathorn, and their two-year-old daughter Betsey, were en route to England when the *Boyd* was captured. Elizabeth was killed – Betsey was one of only four eventual survivors.

take them to safety. But once he got them to shore, Te Pahi was restrained while they were chased and killed. Mrs Morley and the two little girls were taken ashore at the insistence of local women. The ship was then plundered and Te Pahi was offered and accepted three boatloads of goods. Te Ara's people made sure, however, they kept all the guns for themselves. Most stories say the ship caught fire when Te Ara's father, Pipi, testing the firearms, snapped a musket over an opened keg of gunpowder. The powder exploded, killing 13 or 14 Maori on board and setting the *Boyd* alight. It burned fiercely down to the copper-sheathed water line.

The fortunes of the survivors of the massacre were mixed. The journey to Lima in Peru with Berry was made longer by bad weather and the *City of Edinburgh* did not arrive until August. The ship was there for 10 months and during that time Anne Morley died. Her baby daughter and Betsey Broughton were fostered out to families while the cabin boy Thomas Davis was sent on to England. Two years after their rescue, the two girls were returned to Port Jackson. Davis also returned to Sydney. He drowned off New South Wales in 1822. Betsey Broughton was the illegitimate youngest daughter of William Broughton, the deputy commissary at Sydney, who made strenuous efforts to get her back. She later married a wealthy grazier, Charles Throsby, and had 17 children. Today their home is a National Trust property. The fate of Anne Morley's daughter is less clear. Many years later a woman running a school in Sydney claimed to be her, but it was never proved. Berry's bad luck on the trip continued and the *City of Edinburgh* foundered in the Atlantic in 1812 and was finally abandoned off the Azores.

The repercussions from the massacre and burning of the *Boyd* spread through the Bay of Islands and beyond. Te Puna was razed by sailors and many of Te Pahi's people killed. The period of relatively benign relations between the various hapu and tribes in the region was over. Te Pahi was dead within months, along with another of his sons and his fighting chief in a skirmish with a rival at Whangaroa. His friendship with Governor King, and the benefits it brought him, provoked jealousy among local chiefs and proved deadly. His blood line was virtually extinguished and with him went the power of the people at Te Puna. Four years later, Samuel Marsden found the island deserted:

> **"I never passed Tippahee's island without a sigh – it is now desolate, without an inhabitant, and has been so since his death. The ruins of the little cottage, built by the kindness of the late Governor King, still remains and I hope that those Europeans who were engaged in that fatal transaction were ignorant at the time that they were punishing the innocent."**[25]

One day, passing the wreck of the brig lying off shore, Te Ara pointed it out to a group of soldiers travelling on Marsden's vessel *Dromedary* and said, "That's my ship, she is very sorry, she is crying." But, said Richard Cruise their commander, "never once did he express any regret for his horrid crimes…."[26]

Atrocious and Horrible Massacree

"… he gave a dreadful yell, which was the signal for the massacre of the whole ship's company. — There were about 40 in all, 30 of whom the horrid monsters tore limb from limb, and regaled themselves on the flesh of the unfortunate victims. Ten of the men, 2 women passengers, and a lad, ran below; the Chief hailed the men, and told them they had got all they wanted, having plundered the ship, and if they would come down their lives should be spared. The deluded men obeyed, and fell like their comrades, a sacrifice to the inordinate and brutal appetites of the cannibals…."

The Wreck of the ORPHEUS

It was a beautiful summer's morning — clear, sunny and with a fresh breeze blowing. The ship sighted land early and by 8am it had closed to within 65 to 60 kilometres of the shore. As the boilers were stoked, officers and crew studied an unfamiliar landscape:

> "… The coastal range was high and thickly-forested. It seemed to extend southward to the limits of vision; the cliffs were unusually high and steep and, of particular significance to the navigator, there was a seemingly unbroken line of surf beating at their feet which became more and more impressive as the ship came closer to the shore. Such a coast would have appeared daunting enough if the ship was only skirting the shore, but there was the inescapable fact that she had actually to pass through the surf…. [T]he presence of a very considerable area of water beyond the barrier, as indicated in the chart, was a further source of incredulity. This was a strange place indeed…."[1]

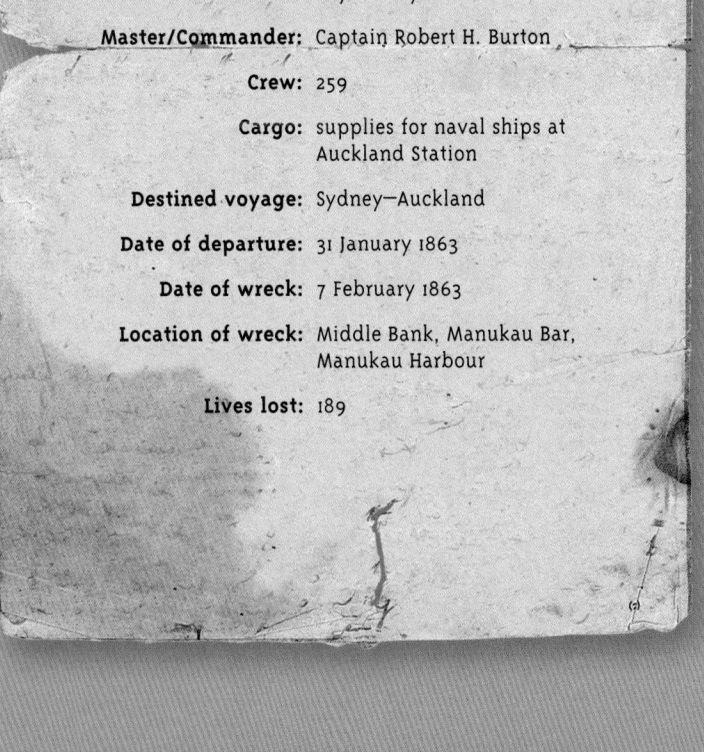

The "strange place" was the Manukau Harbour — an area of 240 square kilometres, at low tide most of it mud and sand banks intersected by dozens of channels, and bounded by 380 kilometres of coastline. High tide covered all the banks, but often not by very much. The most significant and dangerous sand banks were those that acted almost like gates to the harbour's entrance.

HMS Orpheus

Type:	Jason Class 21-gun screw corvette
Built:	Chatham Dockyard
Completed:	October 1861
Length:	69 metres (226 feet 6 inches)
Beam:	12 metres (39 feet 8 inches)
Depth:	7.3 metres (24 feet 2 inches)
Displacement:	2365 tons
Owner:	Royal Navy
Master/Commander:	Captain Robert H. Burton
Crew:	259
Cargo:	supplies for naval ships at Auckland Station
Destined voyage:	Sydney–Auckland
Date of departure:	31 January 1863
Date of wreck:	7 February 1863
Location of wreck:	Middle Bank, Manukau Bar, Manukau Harbour
Lives lost:	189

View of the Manukau Heads

A hand-tinted lithograph by Frederick Rice Stack showing the view from the ranges overlooking the entrance to Manukau Harbour in the early 1860s. Onehunga port was at least an hour's hard riding from Auckland along a rough track.

The ship approaching the harbour entrance was HMS *Orpheus*, a two-year-old, Jason class 21-gun screw corvette in the Royal Navy of 1863. On board was Commodore William Farquharson Burnett C.B., Senior Officer of H.M. Ships and Vessels on the Australian and New Zealand Stations. This was his first visit to New Zealand since taking up his posting in Sydney the previous year. He planned to discuss the deployment of naval vessels and personnel with the Governor, Sir George Grey.

The *Orpheus* had left Sydney early on Saturday 31 January. There was a big crowd to watch it sail: the warship carried a large number of young midshipmen making their first voyage. Burnett headed a crew of 259 officers and men. The ship carried stores and dispatches for the Navy and reinforcements for the war in Taranaki. The Commodore was expected in Auckland on Saturday 7 February. After four days of unfavourable winds, Burnett ordered a change of course and headed for Manukau Harbour to make up time.

At 11.30am on 7 February, the crew was sent below to dinner half an hour early so they would be ready to shorten the sails as soon as needed. Shortly after, the ship's signalman, William Oliert, was called from his meal to check the signal raised on the signal staff on the summit of Paratutai Island at the North Head of the Manukau. It read: "Take the bar", the signal that told incoming ships it was safe to enter the harbour. On the ship's bridge, the commodore, the ship's commander, Robert Heron Burton, and William Strong, the sailing master, bent over their navigation charts. The *Orpheus*'s problems began here.

The treacherous harbour and entrance had been surveyed a number of times in the previous 25 years. The first attempt was done in 1836 by Captain Thomas Wing, now the Manukau pilot and harbour master. That was superseded by a chart mapped by Captain Byron Drury of the Royal Navy, published in January 1856. Five years later, the sailing master of the *Niger* had published a four-page pamphlet, "Veitch's Sailing Instructions", with amended directions for entering the harbour, warning that the Middle Bank at the mouth had shifted north. That same year, Captain Wing also circulated amended instructions for crossing the bar which gave a much wider margin of safety.

Both Veitch's and Wing's new directions were forwarded to the Admiralty and Wing's were also sent directly to the Australian Station at Sydney and published in the *New Zealand Gazette* of August 1861. However, when the *Orpheus* left England in December that year it carried an 1860 chart, Drury's charts with Veitch's Sailing Instructions and an old 1859 copy of *New Zealand Pilot*. When Burnett sailed from Sydney, the ship also carried a copy of the August 1861 *Gazette*, but only as reference for a new set of signals, it seems. Among all those on board, only two men had ever sailed into the Manukau Harbour. One was Edward Amphlett, the paymaster and ship's accountant. The other, Frederick Butler, was a quartermaster from HMS *Harrier*, who had been caught after deserting in Sydney and was being returned under arrest to his ship, now anchored at Onehunga.

Strong, the sailing master, charted his intended course using Veitch's directions but the commodore overrode his decision and insisted they follow Drury's chart to enter the harbour. When they were six kilometres from the bar, William Oliert reported that the signal on Paratutai Island now read "Keep more to north". As the ship closed on the breakers, with sailors at the prow taking regular depth soundings, the commodore, commander and sailing master began another intense discussion about their course. William Strong dared to question Burnett's earlier decision, and this time he prevailed. The order was given to bring the bow round to the north. However, the change of direction was obviously not enough, for the signal remained – keep more to north.

On the summit of Paratutai Island, the acting signalman, Edward Wing, Thomas Wing's son, watched with growing disquiet. "My object was to direct the ship to keep to the northward direction indicated by the arm. The ship did not obey this signal. About a quarter of an hour afterwards the ship bore up and stood direct for the breakers. I let her go on for about a quarter of an hour. She was then about three miles from the breakers. This was about half past one o'clock. I then hauled all the former signals down and hoisted No. 14 signifying 'Keep the vessel more off shore'. This signal was not in any way obeyed."[2]

Meanwhile, on the ship's bridge, a new voice had entered the argument. The deserter Frederick Butler had steered the *Harrier* in the Manukau. He had become so concerned by the ship's position he questioned the decisions of his senior officers. "… I perceived that we were going wrong… at the instance of the crew I went aft and mentioned the danger we were in to the master, Mr Strong. He asked me why I did not come to him before. I replied that I did not know that he was unacquainted with the place. Mr Strong said he was sailing according to his marks on the chart. At this time he was on the bridge

Captain Thomas Wing

Thomas Wing had been harbour master and pilot for five years before the *Orpheus* was wrecked at the Manukau entrance. For weeks after his son and pilot crew searched the coast finding bodies and burying them in the sandhills.

with Commodore Burnett and had the chart in his hand. I pointed out to the Commodore the situation of the channel, who then ordered the helm to be put to starboard. Before this time the ship had touched the ground slightly. About a minute and a half after the order was given to put the helm to starboard the ship struck heavily."[3]

Butler's intervention was too late; and so was Edward Wing's last instruction from the signal station. After reporting the signal to steer a more northerly course, William Oliert recalled, "I saw one signal afterwards, but that was when we were at the entrance of the breakers. It was the stud-arms out [the signal for 'Keep back']. The master gave the order to keep more to port again, and then it was a few seconds after when she struck. I ran aft to dip the ensign, and when I was dipping it she struck."[4]

When the *Orpheus* hit the first time, those on board felt a slight jolt. The order was immediately passed to the engine room to "give her all the steam you can". Some 10 minutes later came the second strike, "not heavily but softly, as if sliding on with her bow. We were then running right before the breakers; she went gradually into it and stopped finally, the rollers following on."[5] The Commodore called "Astern full speed" and "Hands shorten sail", but the momentum of the ship was too great. There was also no response from the engines. The screw did not move. It was either jammed or dislodged. The west coast iron sands gripped the warship fast. Edward Wing, watching from the signal station, did not realise the ship was now aground on the middle bank and kept the "danger" signal aloft. It was approximately 1.40pm.

From then on, there was a rapid and unstoppable progression of events to final disaster. The crew, who had been standing by to shorten sail since 12.30pm, were immediately sent up the masts to lower the topsails and roll up some of the other canvas to try to reduce the impact of the wind on the stationary ship and stabilise it. But even as this was being done, the force of water and wind caused the ship to swing round violently, port side on to the waves, and lurch heavily towards the open sea. The breakers smashed into and over it, ripping away and destroying the second cutter and the jolly boat, the port hammock nettings and port bulwarks and knocking men off their feet. One man was washed overboard and although a lifebuoy was thrown to him he drowned before he could reach it and the buoy broke up in the pounding sea. The hatchways, which had all been battened down when it hit the sand bank, burst open and water poured down below. The windows to the Commodore's cabin, which occupied the whole of the stern on the main deck, shattered before the waves, giving the sea easy entry to the interior of the ship. Burnett ordered the eight port guns, each weighing over three tonnes, to be thrown over the side, but the crew managed to get only four off the ship. As they struggled with the cannons they heard the order "Hands out boats" being piped. Burnett had realised they must abandon ship, but it was to prove an increasingly difficult task.

First he arranged for his desk, papers and the ship's books to be placed in a cutter to be sent ashore. Amphlett had been ordered to the bridge: "Whilst I was on the bridge we saw the smoke of a steamer coming towards us," he recalled. "Shortly after we saw the steamer herself. The Commodore then ordered the starboard cutter to be manned.

Captain Edward Wing

Edward Wing was 21 at the time of the wreck, "nearly six feet high, fully bearded, and not likely to be taken for a boy", he said, denying seeing or speaking to Paymaster Amphlett. The controversy over the loss of the *Orpheus* and the Wings' part in it continued into the 20th century.

The ship was lurching very heavily, the sea breaking right over her. You could not stand on the deck for two minutes at a time…. The boat was lowered [and] shoved off after a great deal of difficulty. Mr Fielding the midshipman was in her. We lost sight of the boat almost the instant she left the ship. The Commodore sent hands up the rigging to see if they could see her. The ebb tide was sweeping her away; there was a very strong tide. We got the pinnace out. The steamer that we had seen, instead of coming towards us, appeared to be going southward. It was that that induced the Commodore to get the big boat out… and [he] ordered me to go in her with Lieutenant Hill to the Head…."[6] Amphlett and Hill were to get help. It was 2.30pm. The tide was halfway out and the men in the cutter and in the pinnace had to row against the force of 240 square kilometres of water pouring out through a relatively narrow and shallow channel. They made painfully slow progress.

Burnett now ordered a 12-metre launch to be made ready. It took 30 crew to get it over the side and tied ready to be lowered. "The Commodore then passed the word, 'Any of the men wishing to save themselves must be ready at the starboard side of ship to jump into the launch '…. About eight hands had obeyed these orders and jumped in…."[7] The first time they tried to let the launch go it got caught under the chains at the front of the ship. With difficulty they pulled it back and tried again. But at the very moment it surged forward, a rogue wave rolled the *Orpheus* to starboard and as it rolled back again the launch was lifted by an anchor fluke which had caught in its gunwale. It capsized, throwing all the men into the sea where most drowned. "The word was then passed to those who could swim, 'Better try and save their lives'," said midshipman Charles Hunt. "The riggings were immediately manned, as it was impossible to stop on deck, the sea breaking right over her."

The wreck's historian Thayer Fairburn gives a graphic picture of conditions for the men on the *Orpheus* at this point:

> "[S]uch was the force of the wind and sea that every wave striking her broadside behaved as though striking a rocky headland, the water exploding upwards and drenching the unfortunate men in the lower rigging even though they were all of 50 feet [15 metres] above the sea. On such a day the waves roll in at about 23 second intervals, three a minute, 180 an hour, and water in such bulk is a very heavy and solid substance, infinitely destructive…."[8]

Moving around in such conditions could be fatal – when John Davy descended from the maintop to the foretop, a coil in a loose stay caught him round the neck and strangled him. Those clinging in the rigging waited for some sign of rescue. It was now about 5pm and for some time they had been trying to gauge the movements of the steamer sighted shortly after the *Orpheus* ran aground. Distance and the rolling seas often hid it from view. After heading south away from them, it had finally noticed their predicament and tried to approach them directly around the middle bank, over the bar

Paymaster Amphlett

Until the end of his life Edward Amphlett maintained that only one signal was flown - "Take the bar" – and that when he called at the signal station he talked to the young signal man who said he thought the ship was simply skirting the reef, as many ships did there.

"The Wreck of the HMS *Orpheus*"

A contemporary painting from 1863 by Richard Brydges. The steamer on the right is the *Wonga Wonga* which towed boats to the wreck. The cutter, in the charge of Midshipman Fielding, is in front. The pinnace in the left foreground (and inset) had Charles Hill at the stern. Hill is standing and wears a life preserver while the solitary figure immediately below the pinnace's bows is the carpenter Beer who managed to keep his cap on all through the wreck.

and up the main channel. But that put the steamer itself in danger. As they watched anxiously it went back along a south channel and for a time they thought it was returning to Onehunga. Then they could see it turn again and head towards them. As the steamer came closer, they saw it was towing the pinnace and the cutter.

The vessel was the coastal steamer *Wonga Wonga* bound for Taranaki. It had left Onehunga in the charge of pilot Thomas Wing shortly after 1pm and taken the south channel out of the harbour, in accordance with Edward Wing's signal. The acting signalman still did not realise the strange ship out at the breakers was in trouble. If he had directed the pilot to take the north channel that would have brought the steamer directly to the stranded warship. On board the *Wonga Wonga* neither the pilot nor its captain, Frederick Renner, who had noted the ship, saw anything wrong. Thomas Wing left the *Wonga Wonga* about 4pm in his whale boat with his pilot's crew – four Maori: Nehana, Timiona, Roma and Kuki. It was only when they had rowed halfway to the signal station that he saw the big ship roll towards land and realised it was aground.

> "I arrived at the Pilot Station [and] shortly afterwards we observed the ship fast settling down with her hull under water, rolling heavily," Wing wrote later. "I then manned the pilot-boat and started for the wreck, and when abreast of the Orwell Shoal saw two boats with crews in them in the breakers on the shoal. I then waved the Pilot Flag to conduct them out of danger...."[9]

The pinnace's and cutter's crews had been rowing for two hours against the outgoing tide and had covered not much more than one and a half kilometres. Edward Amphlett described what happened next. "When we met with Mr Wing we asked him if he had communicated with the *Harrier* or town, and he said that no communication could be made and that in fact there was nobody to send. We asked him about a lifeboat and he said that it would take 12 men two days to get it down."[10]

They decided the pilot's whaleboat would make faster time than the pinnace and that Amphlett, being familiar with the area, should go on to Onehunga to get assistance. Lieutenant Charles Hill continued: "The cutter now came up with us, Mr Wing and his Maoris came into the pinnace, while Mr Amphlett, two sick men and two boys and two others started off in the whaler to the *Harrier*. We pushed on to the steamer [the *Wonga Wonga*], now between the Heads, waving, signalling and making every effort to get her attention. After some delay she turned round and closed us, taking pinnace and cutter in tow, proceeding to the wreck which we reached at 6pm. I found her lying very much over to port, the masts all standing, the crew in the rigging above the tops, the sea at times sweeping as high as the futtock rigging."[11]

Captain Renner now had to manoeuvre the *Wonga Wonga* with great finesse if he was not to endanger it as well. He towed the cutter and pinnace to within 60 metres up wind of the *Orpheus* and then let them go. They drifted down until they were about 25 to 35 metres from the starboard bow of the wreck. Commodore Burnett called to those in the bowsprit and jib-boom to jump. The sea below them was less turbulent. The pinnace managed to pick up seven or eight men before their boat drifted beyond the wreck. According to Charles Hunt not all were so lucky: "Others jumped off the starboard beam and quarter of the ship, trying to swim for the boats, but were unable to fetch them."[12]

The remaining guns had begun to tear loose and crash about as the ship wallowed in the breakers. In the sea around them was a growing amount of wreckage. The men could only move forward towards the bow by the masts and rigging. The deck, below water, had been unusable for some time. William Burnett now shouted to the men above the roar of wind and wave, "Every one of you is to say his prayers and look out for himself. I will be the last. The Lord have mercy on us all." Below them, the men in the cutter and pinnace called out, encouraging them to jump and swim for the boats.

"Having drifted to leeward, the steamer came and towed me to windward," Charles Hill recounted the following day. "I dropped down a second time with the cutter in company. This time, three or four men were taken in the pinnace and the boatswain and four or five men in the cutter. It was now about 7 o'clock. The flood tide had made. The rollers soon became very high and dangerous on the change. The jib-boom broke off short by the cap. It was quite impossible with safety to the boats to remain any longer by the wreck. As I was going back I shouted to the wreck to make a final attempt, but none would venture."[13]

The steamer picked up the two smaller boats and anchored just over a kilometre away. It was 8pm and night was closing in. The *Wonga Wonga* lit blue lights and began blowing its steam whistle and ringing the ship's bell to give its position. Some time between 8pm and 8.30pm, the masts fell and with them over a hundred men crowded into the rigging. The pinnace and cutter set out again for the wreck. A legend has grown that as the masts tore loose the sound of "three heart-rending farewell cheers" went up; but Harbour Pilot Thomas Wing remembered hearing only "the screams of men being launched into eternity".[14] Charles Hunt was one of the very few to survive.

> "At about 8.30pm the mainmast went, carrying with it the foretopmast and Commander Burton, Lieutenant Mudge, Mr Story the master, Mr Broughton, midshipman, myself, and about 50 hands…. Commander Burton was seen with his head between the shrouds, which jammed his head and throat between them, killing him instantly…. The mainmast went first, then the foremast and then the mizzenmast…. When the mizzenmast went [Commodore Burnett] was between the top and the futtock rigging, the former of which fell on his head partly stunning him. He rose up once, and seemed to make no effort to save himself, and was lost….
>
> "I was holding on the futtock rigging about 20 minutes, and the seas washing right over us. At intervals of five minutes a sea would come and wash alternatively over and under where I was holding on by. Twice I

was washed away from where I was holding on, the next sea bringing me back again. The last time I could recognise any men on the top with me, I saw four. A heavy sea then came and washed me off, and carried the remaining officers away. I found myself being taken by the tide fast away from the ship towards the shore, and supported myself for several miles with a capstan bar, having had two very hard knocks on the head with timber as the waves came rolling over. I saw two people in the water near me, but could not recognise them. One was on the top of a chest of drawers, as far as I can make out. I then heard them singing out to the boat to save them. I looked in the direction they were going and I saw the first cutter taking in one of those men. I immediately hailed her, was answered and picked up."[15]

After checking for more survivors and finding none, Wing's Maori crew manning the cutter took the men to shore and then to their hut where they gave them food and bedding. Later some of the sailors went back to the beach to see whether any bodies had washed up on the incoming tide, but all they found was "a chest of tea, a cask of peas, a case of candles, and the Commodore's cot with all the bedding on it". Charles Hill in the pinnace had also found some who survived the masts' collapse. "The pinnace picked up six or eight and returned to the steamer with one or two in the last stages of exhaustion. On again nearing the wreck I found the ship completely broken up. It was a beautiful clear moonlight night and masses of the wreck kept passing in with the flood, clinging to which Lieutenant Yonge and six or eight men were saved. The cutter got so far to leeward that she made for land, the pinnace returning to the steamer. We remained on deck the whole night keeping a sharp lookout. At daylight nothing could be seen of the ill-fated *Orpheus* but the stump of one mast and a few ribs."[16]

At first light, the *Wonga Wonga* circled the wreck area and then anchored on the south bank of the river inside Puponga Point, up harbour from North Head. The steamer *Avon* came alongside at 6.30am with Edward Amphlett on board. After failing to find anyone to pilot him to Onehunga, Amphlett and his small crew had made good time on the 27 kilometres up the harbour, more than half that time rowing against the outgoing tide and then the last two hours in darkness.

Of the 259 men who set out from Sydney, just 69 were rescued – eight officers and 61 petty officers, seamen, marines and boys. Of those lost in the shipwreck, only a third were found and buried, usually where they were discovered. The bodies of Commodore Burnett and Chief Boatswain's Mate John Pascoe were brought back to Auckland and buried there. Burnett received full military honours – his corpse drawn on a gun carriage by 16 survivors of the *Orpheus* in a funeral procession that set out as 20-minute guns were fired. Those who died had sailed over 30,000 kilometres from England only to drown within three kilometres of land, and 15 minutes from safe water. It was inevitable there would be questions, accusations and efforts made to apportion blame.

There were three major inquiries and a number of reports. From the outset, the

Commodore Burnett

A painting of Commodore William Farquharson Burnett in naval uniform by Thayer Fairburn, *Orpheus* historian. Burnett was born in Scotland and went to sea at 13. He rose through the ranks, was mentioned in Dispatches during the Crimean War and awarded a number of military honours. Although officially exonerated of the wreck of the *Orpheus*, several senior naval officers thought he should not have attempted to enter the harbour without a pilot, and was wrong to have interfered with the navigation of the ship.

SHIPWRECK

Royal Navy took the position that none of its officers and men could be at fault. The first inquiry was held two days after HMS *Orpheus* was wrecked, before representatives of the colonial administration on board HMS *Miranda* in Auckland Harbour. It came to an abrupt and unsatisfactory conclusion when a senior officer tried to stop proceedings and officers from the *Orpheus* refused to continue answering questions. There were arguments over the accuracy of some evidence and, most surprisingly, the Wings and Frederick Butler were not called to give their version of events.

They were, however, present on 16 and 23 February for the Coroner's Inquest into the cause of death of John Pascoe. Pascoe's body had been found north of the Pilot Station by Thomas Wing. But this was an inquiry with limited powers. The Coroner's jury concluded that Pascoe had died by drowning in the wreck of the *Orpheus* and the circumstances that caused it "ought to be enquired into by the Authorities of the Colony". A Select Committee was specially set up but its drawn-out investigations were inconclusive – it did not apportion blame or exonerate any of those involved.

While the Select Committee was still sitting, the British Admiralty held its own court martial. It took place on board the *Victory*, Lord Nelson's old ship, on 27 April 1863 at Portsmouth. Two days before, an article had appeared in the *Naval and Military Gazette* criticising the questioning of Commodore Burnett's judgement and actions and urging, "De mortuis nil nisi bonum" – think nothing but good of the dead. Once again Butler was not called and there was no statement from Thomas or Edward Wing. The court named as the causes of the disaster "the Bar having shifted, and the absence of all Pilot Boats and efficient means to denote the exact position of the Banks and depth of water over the Bar rendering navigation peculiarly difficult".[17] The Commodore and his officers and crew were acquitted of blame and commended for their discipline and courage.

On 22 May that year, the Secretary to the Admiralty Hydrographer, A.B. Becher, also published a report on the ship's loss. From the very first inquiry on board the *Miranda*, Thomas Wing realised that he and his son were the likely and convenient scapegoats. Now Becher laid the blame unequivocally on the Wings, the ambiguity of the signals raised and the unsatisfactory state of the signal station.

The Wings had already faced hostility from the press, local government and some survivors. It was ironic that several of the inadequacies highlighted by Becher had already been raised by Wing in a regular exchange of letters with the Auckland Superintendent dating back several years before the wreck of the *Orpheus*. After the wreck, the Provincial Council belatedly ordered a report on the Pilot Station at Manukau Heads.

Although Thomas Wing had to continue to fight for funds to improve the safety of the harbour and its constantly shifting bar, there were improvements, and in 1874 the first kerosene oil-powered light in New Zealand was erected at the Heads. HMS *Orpheus* was not the last ship to come to grief in the Manukau Harbour. There have been many vessels, stranded, damaged and lost since, but none has cost so many lives. More than a century later, the *Orpheus* still has the dubious distinction of being the New Zealand shipwreck in which the greatest number of people died – 189.

Captain William Renner of the *Wonga Wonga*

Captain Renner put his own ship at risk to try and save some of the crew of the *Orpheus*. Above right is a letter from Lieutenant Charles Hill, one of the few survivors. It was written from the HMS *Curacod* and is dated 5 October 1863. It reads:

" The surviving officers of the HMS Sailing Ship *Orpheus* request Captain Renner to accept the accompanying present — a Pencil Case in proof of the high esteem and regard with which they will [?] remember the considerable kindness of himself and ship crew to them on the 7 of Feb. 1863. I remain Dear Sir yours sincerely Charles Hill."

The Wreck of the DELAWARE
– Huria's Story

In 1863, at the height of the New Zealand Wars, the citizens of Nelson gathered to formally thank and reward five Maori from a neighbouring pa who had risked their lives to save 10 men during a shipwreck. The award ceremony became a political opportunity. Newspapers, Government and judiciary used the rescue as an illustration of good and co-operative citizenry and told the Maori heroes that the settlers accorded more respect and admiration to the selfless saving of lives than the exploits of any great warrior.

The wreck and rescue had occurred in the early spring of 1863, during one of the worst gales those on the Nelson coast had ever experienced. The vessel was the *Delaware*, a pretty brigantine of 241 tons, built in Nova Scotia specifically for trade in the colonies, and still on its maiden voyage. The master, Captain Robert Baldwin, had a 50 per cent ownership of the ship. The other 50 per cent was owned by Green Robinson & Company of Fenchurch Street, London, and insured with the underwriters Lloyd's. Baldwin's share was uninsured. The vessel had left Gravesend for New Zealand with 101 tonnes of general

The Delaware

Type:	brigantine
Built:	Ives Shipping Yard, Nova Scotia, Canada, 1862
Length:	35.5 metres (117 feet)
Beam:	7.8 metres (25 feet 9 inches)
Depth:	3.4 metres (11 feet 4 inches)
Tonnage:	241 tons net
Port of registry:	London
Owner:	Green Robinson & Company of Fenchurch Street, London, and Captain Robert C. Baldwin
Master:	Captain Robert C. Baldwin
Crew:	10
Passengers:	one
Cargo:	approx 101.6 tonnes general cargo
Destined voyage:	London–New Zealand
Date of departure:	9 April 1863
Date of wreck:	4 September 1863
Location of wreck:	Delaware Bay (then Whakapuaka Bay), Nelson
Lives lost:	one

SHIPWRECK

A ship in trouble
The taxing rescue from the wreck to the shore along a single cable and through angry seas inspired artists of the time.

cargo on 9 April 1863. Four months later, it berthed in Nelson where it unloaded some of the cargo. At 11am on Thursday 3 September, they left Nelson on the last leg of the trip. As well as a crew of 10, the brig carried a single passenger, Henry Lufkin Skeet, a surveyor on his way home to Napier, the *Delaware*'s final destination.

Although the weather was fine, the wind was against them and they had to tack out of the harbour. By nightfall, they still had not cleared Tasman Bay and the wind was strengthening. Over the next few hours with the wind shifting from north to north-east and back to north and the seas rising, the ship continued to tack across the bay, Baldwin taking soundings every half-hour to check his position. By 1am on Friday, it was raining heavily and the wind had reached gale force. While Henry Skeet stayed below, all hands were busy on deck. It was so dark, the weather "thick as a hedge" according to the captain, that they could not see the Nelson light. Unable to make for a safe anchorage, Baldwin hove to for a couple of hours. At 4 o'clock in the morning, they thought they saw land. "We saw a thick cloud before us and wore ship in consequence. We could not go about because we were under a close-reefed topsail. It was raining heavily. We were driven so close to the land, while lying-to, that we could not get away."[1]

Several times during the night, the captain had asked his passenger about the lie of the coastline. Now at daybreak, with the wind blowing violently in shore, he saw he was off Whakapuaka Bay, about 25 kilometres from Nelson. A local paper's description sounds far from welcoming:

> "…a little bay formed by the running in of the coast from Graham's Point round to Pepin's Island which lies close to the coast…. Not far from the island is a strip of sandy beach, apparently about three-quarters of a mile in extent. The rest of the coast all along to Graham's Point is precipitous and rockbound, with large boulders lying about, and numerous sunken rocks."[2]

The captain tried first and without success to make for the shelter of Pepin's Island. Next he attempted to reach and pass round the Croisilles, but he lost the jib and failed again. The ship was now even further inshore. Baldwin had already warned Henry Skeet that their predicament was serious: "Between four and five o'clock on Friday morning the captain… called me and told me I had better get together my things I wanted to save; and then I went on deck and he told me to cut away the life buoys from the stern and take charge of them and place them on the companion stairs, so that I might be ready to hand them if anyone was washed overboard."[3]

The ship's master now ordered the small bower anchor dropped. Although they were in 13 fathoms of water, they ran out 90 fathoms of anchor chain before the windlass broke under the strain. A second anchor was dropped immediately. It was plain to Baldwin they would not get clear of the shore and he did not think the second anchor would hold any better in such enormous seas. He began looking for a sandy place to beach his ship. It was then that the cable to the second anchor parted. As Henry Skeet watched, the captain "then made sail and put a man at the wheel and tried to run her ashore on the beach, but finding himself unable to do so he put her stem on to the nearest point, putting her before the wind so as to save her being dashed to pieces broadside on the rocks". His efforts were in vain. The ship got among the huge rollers and could not be steered. Shortly after 8.30am, she struck a large boulder some 130 to 180 metres from the shore and became stuck on submerged rocks. The huge seas now beat down on the stranded vessel. The two lifeboats were soon washed away and smashed. The men had to find a way off the ship if they were to survive. The mate, Henry Squirrell, volunteered to take a line and swim for the shore.

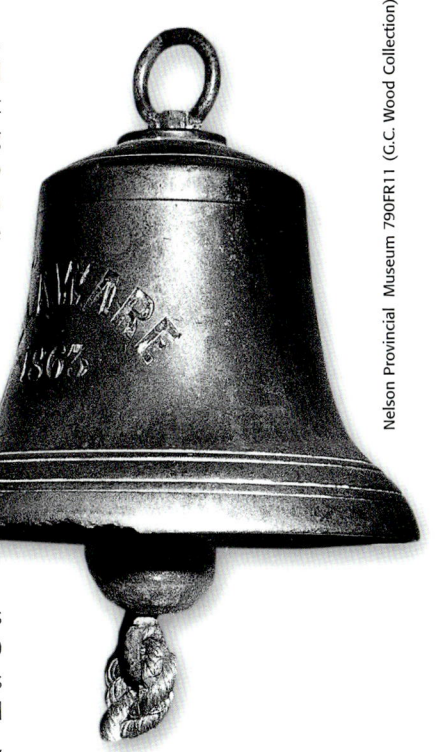

Squirrell was a 26-year-old merchant seaman from Suffolk. His father was a watchmaker and when Henry left school at 12 he began an apprenticeship in watchmaking, intending to join the family business. However, Henry hankered after a more exciting and adventurous life and 10 years later he decided to exchange horology for a career at sea. His ambition was to become a first mate in the merchant navy, and it was as chief mate that Captain Baldwin employed him for the *Delaware*'s first

The Wreck of the
DELAWARE
– Huria's Story

Nelson Provincial Museum 790FR11 (G.C. Wood Collection)

The ship's bell
For many years, the bell from the *Delaware* punctuated the school day for the children of Appleby School. It nows hangs in Nelson Provincial Museum.

commercial voyage. When they reached Nelson, Squirrell became ill and had to be admitted to Nelson Hospital. He was there for two weeks before he returned to work on the ship.

On board the stranded vessel, able seaman William Morgan stood by to help Squirrell. "The mate, who was a good swimmer, thought he could swim ashore, and took the lead line and tied it round his waist, and lowered himself into the water by going down the martingale [the stay holding down the jib-boom] of the ship. In going down he struck his back against the rock, and he sang out 'Oh the rock, oh the rock!' and could not come up again. I saw this and heard him cry out as I was on the bow at the time clearing away the line for him…. [He] was not in the water when he struck the rock, but he fell into the water immediately after, and then floated to the main chains. Two buoys were thrown to him by the captain, but he could not catch either…. When we lifted him out of the water… the line was round his feet and by that we lifted him. He was helpless and senseless, and was all of a heap."[4]

Henry Skeet joined the crew on deck while they tried to revive the injured and unconscious man by rubbing him briskly. Skeet heard Squirrell cry out "just as a dying man would call out", then there was no response. Captain and crew "gave him up for dead, for we did not think there was any life in him. We laid him in the forecastle in one of the bunks."[5] As the huge seas continued to pound the ship, the crew caught sight of a small group of Maori running towards them along the shore. Members of the pa at Whakapuaka overlooking the bay had seen the ship in the gloomy dawn as the crew fought to escape the bay and then tried unsuccessfully to beach the brigantine. As the ship was driven ever closer to the shore, a young woman and four men raced the one and a half kilometres from the pa down to the shore.

Skeet was the only one on board who spoke Maori. Above the roar of the storm he shouted to them that the only way off the ship now was by a rope secured to the shore. "I directed Morgan to stand by with the lead line and told the Maoris to look out for it. The line was thrown and the Maoris rushed into the water and caught it…." The lead line was caught by Hohapata Kahupuku, a man known for his incredible strength. Together with 22-year-old Huria Matenga and her husband, Hemi, he struggled back to shallow waters. Meanwhile the crew attached a heavy cable to the lead line and Hohapata dragged it in through the boiling surf. Eraia Te Rei helped him tie the thick rope round a large rock while the other end was fastened to the *Delaware*'s foremast. As the crew prepared to abandon ship, the oldest of the group on shore, Kerei Te Rei, began building a bonfire on the sand.

Henry Squirrell

Henry left school at 12 to begin an apprenceship in watchmaking but hankered after a more exciting life and decided on a career at sea.

Even with the cable in place, the route to the foreshore and safety was still perilous. Baldwin and William Morgan estimated they had run out about 100 fathoms [about 180 metres] of new rope from the *Delaware* to the boulder. As the ship rolled and pitched in the breakers, their lifeline sagged beneath the waves and snapped taut in the air. They went down it one at a time. Morgan went first. Skeet was fourth off the ship. Baldwin anxiously watched his men: "The surf was very heavy and breaking regularly over the vessel, which was lurching to and fro with each sea, greatly endangering the rope which was slacked occasionally to meet the lurches, as each man descended. Several were struck on the rocks in their perilous descent, but the Maoris, Julia [Huria] the readiest of them all, rushed into the surf up to the neck and often enveloped by the breakers, and seized each man as he neared, and thus saved the lives of many who from exhaustion could not have otherwise got to the shore."[6]

When all his crew were safely on dry land, Baldwin went forward to the forecastle to check Henry Squirrell one last time. The ship now lay with her keel out of the water and he could hear the others shouting that the cable had started to fray and part and would soon break. He said later that the first mate lay "his mouth open, his eyes fixed and glassy, and his body motionless".[7] The captain thought him "quite dead" and abandoned his ship. Several times as he struggled along the hawser it slackened and submerged him; then he was smashed on rocks and lost consciousness. When he came to, he was lying beside the fire Kerei had kindled on the shore. The three Maori – Huria, Hemi and Hohapata – in one last dash into the stormy seas, had pulled him to safety as the cable finally gave way. William Morgan said the captain "cried like a child" at the loss of his ship and its first mate.

It had taken an hour for the 10 men to get ashore. The Maori laid them round the fires to warm and recover and brought them food. They had begun to take some of the crew up to the pa to better shelter when those left on the beach noticed movement on the ship. To their shock and horror they saw the first mate working his way across the deck to the fore-rigging. The ship was still on her side. He shouted to them to come and get him. Henry Skeet begged the Maori to go out and bring Squirrell in as he, more than any of them, could not make it by himself. "They said they could do nothing till the tide went down," he recalled sadly. "The tide was then rising and a fearful surf was rolling in which washed right over the vessel. I made signs to the mate to lash himself to the rigging. Soon after the mainmast gave way and being afraid of the foremast going lest it carry him overboard, I made signs for him to go aft. While he went aft I stood in

Nelson Provincial Museum 81992/3-1/2 (Tyree Studio Collection)

Hohapata Kahupuku

Kahupuku was one of five Maori from the pa at Whakapuaka who braved huge waves to rescue the crew. He received a £50 reward from the Government.

SHIPWRECK

the water, having a life buoy, and holding on by a rope, the other end of which was held by the steward, so as to assist him if he should fall."[8]

The mate made it to the main rigging and, standing on the outside of the ship, managed with difficulty to get his arms over the rigging. Those on shore shouted to him to hold on. When the tide ebbed they would come out for him. "I called to him, 'Cheer up, and hold on for one other hour and you will be saved'," said Henry Skeet. "I watched him for quarter of an hour and then left him to go and speak with the captain who was lying exhausted beside the fire. I had just gone away when Julia [Huria] said, 'The Pakeha has let go.' I looked round and [Squirrell] was gone."[9] Although Skeet watched the waves and beach, there was no sign of the mate. A couple of hours later, under the strain of the relentless seas, the *Delaware* broke up. As Baldwin observed, "Neither boat, canoe nor ship could live in such a gale and such a sea."

After the Maori helped the remaining crew members up to the pa, Hemi Matenga rode into Nelson that afternoon to give the ship's agents, N. Edwards & Co, news of the wreck and to get assistance. The following morning, the steamer *Lyttelton* took an agent of the company round to Whakapuaka Bay to see what could be salvaged. It was a desolate sight:

> "The wreck now lies at the foot of a precipitous cliff, from 350 to 400 feet [100 to 120 metres] high; and here the rocks and boulders lie in great numbers. The vessel is cut completely in half, her stern part, with the stump of the main mast still standing, is about 25 or 30 yards from the face of the cliff, while some 15 yards to the left lies the fore part, half split up, the ribs exposed, the decks smashed in, and the timbers in many places snapt [sic] as if cut by a saw.
> "Everything was swept from the poop, and the deck towards the mainmast was bent down and fallen in. Below, the cabin is in a frightful confusion, the doors of the sleeping cabins being smashed and broken, the furniture destroyed, and everything except the overturned stove appearing to have been emptied out amidships, or fallen into the hold through the lower deck. All around the beach for at least three miles [five kilometres] are strewn boxes, barrels, blankets, shawls, candles, innumerable tins of fancy biscuits, full and empty, and the debris of many packages of grocery, saddlery, drapery and other goods mingled with fragments of the wreck, splintered in many instances into small pieces. A small mahogany harmonium is lying near the wreck, its keys exposed and its sides smashed and broken."[10]

About one and a half kilometres from the wreck and among the wreckage, they found the body of the first mate. He still wore his sea boots; his clothes were pulled up over his head. Robert Baldwin cut them away to identify him and then helped carry him up out of reach of the tide. The *Lyttelton* returned to Nelson on Sunday carrying all the cargo that could be saved and Squirrell's body. That same day nearly 200 locals cruised over to have a look at the wreck site on the steamer *Sturt*.

Two inquiries were held into the mate's death: the first by the shipping agent Nathaniel Edwards on the beach adjacent to the wreck on Saturday afternoon; the second, a full coroner's inquest in Nelson at 2pm on Monday 7 September. Morgan and Skeet said that the captain had done everything possible to save the ship and his men. The captain, crew and their passenger all testified that they believed Squirrell was dead before they left the *Delaware*. George Williams, a Nelson surgeon, made an external examination of the body:

> "There are slight abrasions on the back of the hands and knees. The skin of the face is much discoloured and decomposition is commencing. There are some small wounds made by shells on the forehead. I removed portions of shell from the wounds. There is no fracture of any bone of the extremities, or of the spinal column. Both hands were clenched and contained a quantity of straw, seaweed and sand. He had heavy sea-boots on reaching to his knees. His trousers were off and his drawers were drawn downwards over his feet. He had on two Crimean shirts and a blue one which were inside out and were entangled and hung by the wristbands of the sleeves only to his hands. His body was naked except the hanging drawers and his boots. I think he endeavoured to strip himself. I fancy, from the description I have heard here, that when drawn up on board he was suffering from exhaustion."[11]

As there was no serious wound on the body that would have killed him, and as the doctor believed the abrasion on Squirrell's forehead happened after he died, he had little doubt the cause of death was drowning. At the end of both hearings, the juries returned a verdict of accidental drowning, "and that such a death was caused principally by injury or exhaustion sustained while courageously endeavouring to swim ashore with a line in order to save the rest of the crew...."[12] The end came without fanfare two days later. Henry Squirrell's funeral left Albion Wharf on 9 September at 1.30pm, a bare half hour before the shipping agents began an auction for the salvaged cargo there. He was buried in the Anglican block of the Whakapuaka Cemetery. No headstone was raised to mark his grave.

In the course of the hearings into the death of Henry Squirrell, those who testified had paid tribute to their five rescuers from the Whakapuaka pa. They believed all lives would have been lost without their extraordinary efforts to help. The young woman, Huria, was repeatedly singled out for special mention. Huria was born at Hawaiki on Mahei-puku (Pepin's Island) some time between 1840 and 1842, of Te Atiawa, Ngati Tama and Ngati Toa descent. She could trace her ancestry back to the Tokomaru canoe. Her maternal grandfather was Henare Te Keha, Chief of Te Atiawa. Her father's father was a renowned

Nelson Provincial Museum 59206/3-1/2 (Tyree Studio Collection)

Hemi Matenga

Hemi Matenga was the son of Metapere Wai-punahau of Kapiti and George Stubbs, whaler, trader and substantial landowner in the Waikanae district. He was an astute businessman and with his wife, Huria, profitably leased land she had inherited to Pakeha farmers. They had one adopted daughter, Mamae.

Huria Matenga

Huria Matenga had considerable mana in the Pakeha and Maori communities. She was praised by the former for her bravery and beauty, and was treated as a local celebrity. Her tribal affiliations and land held in Taranaki, Porirua and Nelson meant she travelled widely, arranging marriages, naming children and taking an interest in family matters. Among the guests who stayed at the Matenga's large homestead were the prophets Te Whiti and Tohu, Bishop Suter and Alexander Mackay, later Native Land Court judge.

warrior and the Ngati Tama leader, Te Puoho-o-te-rangi. However, her parents, Wikitoria Te Amohau Te Keha of Ngati Te Whiti and Wiremu Katene Te Puoho, had become followers of the pacifist teachings of Te Whiti-o-Rongomai III and Tohu Kakahi. When Huria was 17, she married Hemi Matenga Wai-punahau of the Ngati Toa at the Christ Church Cathedral in Nelson. It was an arranged marriage neither of them wanted.

On Saturday 14 November, the local people packed the Nelson Provincial Hall for a special presentation ceremony. The coroner's jury had recommended that some "substantial testimony" should be given to Huria, Hemi and Hohapata by the Government. However, it was felt that a public appeal would be more meaningful and show the gratitude of the people of Nelson. By November they had raised over £62. With the money they bought five pocket watches and chains, one in gold for Huria and the other four in silver.

In the presentation address, Huria's "intrepid conduct" was likened to the young British heroine Grace Darling, a lighthouse keeper's daughter who had helped her father save passengers and crew from a shipwreck one stormy night. "And like her, Julia, your name and deed will find a place in local history. Your brave act is one of which a queen might be proud, and we present you with a watch whereon your children and their successors may read with pleasure an inscription which testifies the esteem in which you are held by the settlers of Nelson." The engraved text read:

> "Na nga tangata o Whakatu (kia Huria) he tohu. Whakamoemiti mo tona maiatanga ki te whakaora i nga tangata o te Terawera, 4 Hepetema, 1863."

On the other side of the case was the English translation:

> "Presented to Julia, by the settlers of Nelson, in recognition of her heroism at the rescue of the crew of the Delaware, 4th September, 1863."

Each of the men received an address with their watch. Hemi Matenga's read in part:

> "...Englishmen know no distinction when rewarding conspicuous merit.... Mankind – no matter what colour or race – are knit together by the feelings of our common nature and, displaying as you did the highest attributes of humanity on the occasion which this commemorates, you have made yourself worthy of the recognition of all noble-minded men by your praiseworthy deed...."

The five also received a reward from the colonial Government on the recommendation of the Governor, Sir George Grey. Huria and Hemi Matenga and Hohapata Kahupuku were each given £50 and Eraia and Kerei Te Rei £10. It was hoped that they would accept the money "not in the light of a money payment for the service they had performed, but as an evidence of the gratitude of the Government for their good and

Huria's funeral

When Huria Matenga died on 24 April 1909, her status and achievements, and her heroic role in the rescue of the *Delaware*'s crew, gained her a place in Maori and Pakeha folklore.

Nelson Provincial Museum C1123

Christian act of saving life, even at the risk of their own". Hemi Matenga's reply was greeted with loud cheers: "On behalf of myself and the others I will say that we are much pleased at this mark of the esteem and regard of the people of Nelson. We had no idea, at the time we saved the Europeans' lives, of receiving any reward. We heard their cry for help and we assisted them."[13]

Modern historians have found the symbolism of the award irresistible: "The heroism of Huria Matenga and her kin could not be divorced from other concerns, at least in the eyes of settler opinion. The *Nelson Examiner* took the opportunity to note the noble intentions of the Government in prosecuting the Waikato war. At the same time, by recognising heroism, it could be shown that 'where the colonists, by their numbers, have power to restrain disorder, they also have the will and ability to recognise good citizens'. A reward was thus to be recommended, but it should not be so large that 'the weakness of the Maori – his covetousness – should be stimulated'."[14]

As predicted, Huria remained extremely well known until her death in April 1909. About 2000 Maori and Pakeha attended her tangi at her large homestead overlooking the renamed Delaware Bay. She was buried with her parents and other iwi of high rank in the urupa called Haua opposite Pepin's Island. Hemi died three years later and was buried beside her.

William Morgan, able seaman on the *Delaware*, did not return to his native London. He stayed on in New Zealand living in Dunedin and working on coastal ships until his death in 1888. Henry Skeet had been surveying the Napier and Nelson districts in the early 1860s. The year after the wreck he joined the New Zealand Wars. He helped recruit a corps of engineers to take part in the Bay of Plenty campaign. When the fighting was over he was employed to survey the confiscated land at Tauranga. In 1872, he moved with his staff to Taranaki where he was in charge of surveying the confiscated land in South Taranaki. Soon after he became chief surveyor for the Land Purchase Department. He was working for the department when he died in 1882.

Back in England, one of Henry Squirrell's younger relations was called "Baldwin", a name that appears nowhere else in the family. Later generations have wondered at that coincidence. Is it possible that Robert Baldwin felt the need to atone for the death of his chief mate and that after his return to England he helped support various members of Henry Squirrell's family? They are inclined to think so.

The Wreck of the
DELAWARE
– Huria's Story

The Matenga Homestead

Hemi Matenga enjoyed the life of an English squire. He and Huria entertained on a grand scale at their homestead overlooking Delaware Bay, surrounded by extensive lawns, gardens and a tennis court.

Nelson Provincial Museum 179465/3 (Tyree Studio Collection)

ATL G-016396-1/2 (De Maus Collection)

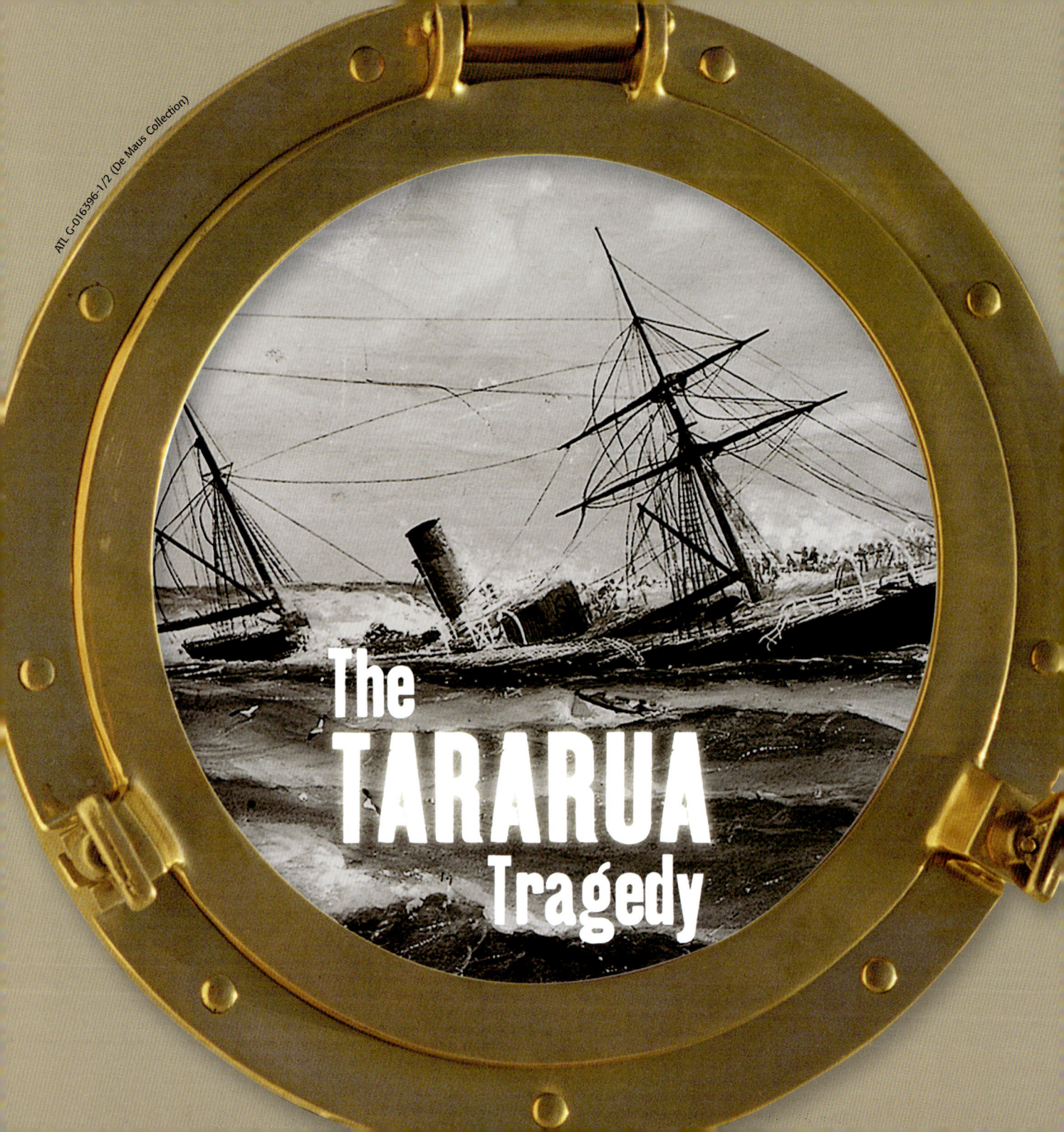

The TARARUA Tragedy

Over the years, there have been many stories about what took place. People said the entire crew were roaring drunk, that passengers danced and sang on the decks as they waited to be rescued, that the sea was glassy calm at the time and the water where they went aground so shallow everyone could have walked to safety. The truth was far less carnival; the circumstances much less benign. But getting the story wrong was part of the SS *Tararua* tragedy.

The first brief report: "… all lives safe the vessel close in shore" gave the wrong impression and removed any urgency from rescue attempts. When slightly fuller versions were published the following day, those terse few words had been expanded – "No lives are lost, all passengers and crew having been landed safely on shore." In the parlance of the day, the newspaper report created little "excitement" and lulled public concern. The reality was very different. Instead, the *Tararua* was to become the worst civilian shipping catastrophe in New Zealand's history.

The SS *Tararua* was a favourite of the colony's travelling public in the late 1800s. An iron-screw steamer built at Dundee in Scotland in 1864, it was considered fast for its class at that time. The Union Steam Ship Company was its third owner, having bought the four transtasman vessels

SS Tararua

Type:	iron-screw steamer
Built:	Gourlay Brothers & Company, Dundee, Scotland, 1864
Length:	67.67 metres (222 feet 6 inches)
Beam:	8.53 metres (28 feet)
Depth:	4.88 metres (16 feet 2 inches)
Tonnage:	828 tons gross, 563 tons net register, an increase during alterations
Machinery:	two direct-acting engines of 155 n.h.p.
Owner:	Union Steam Ship Company, Dunedin
Master:	Captain Francis George Garrard
Crew:	40
Passengers:	111
Cargo:	large general cargo including live geese and pigs, 70 bales of flax, 300 bags of barley, 2 tanks of malt, 250 casks of lime juice, mail, a consignment of specially boxed cheese (a trial export), and 8 to 10 tonnes of general goods; also an estimated £4000 worth of silver coins for re-minting
Destined voyage:	Port Chalmers–Melbourne, via Hobart
Date of departure:	28 April 1881
Date of wreck:	29 April 1881
Location of wreck:	Otara Reef off Waipapa Point at the north-east end of Foveaux Strait
Lives lost:	131

Captain Francis Garrard

Francis Garrard was well known among the travelling public. Newspapers and magazines described him as "dashing" while his employers considered him "a zealous officer and a strict abstainer".

Otago Settlers Museum SC193

belonging to McMeckan, Blackwood in 1878. The *Tararua* had been kept up to date. It was strengthened, new engines and boilers were fitted, cabin accommodation was increased and the saloon enlarged. The £8000 refit made it one of the "better appointed and more comfortable steamboats"[1] on the Australasian passenger-cargo routes. The steamer went into service for its new owners on what was known as the "long trip" – from Melbourne, round the New Zealand coast and then back via Hobart. Passengers liked it because it had a reputation for punctuality. In the often uncertain days of sea travel, the *Tararua* kept to its timetable.

In mid-April 1881, the ship had made a crossing from Sydney, arriving at Russell on April 17 after a four-day voyage. It stopped next in Auckland and left there on April 21 to begin its run down to the southern ports before returning to Hobart and Melbourne. When it cast off from the Railway Pier at its home port, Port Chalmers, at 5pm on Thursday 28 April, and sailed out past the Heads on a full tide 40 minutes later, the *Tararua* had only one more local port of call – Bluff – before heading into the Tasman for Hobart. The vessel was carrying a crew of 40, 111 passengers and a valuable cargo including £4000 of silver coins.

The voyage began normally enough. The master and crew had only recently been transferred to the *Tararua* after a much publicised scandal when a £5000 box of gold bars went missing during a Tasman crossing. Although it was not found,[2] the ship's former captain and the entire crew were reassigned to other vessels in the fleet. At the same time, Captain Francis Garrard was without a vessel after a collision with a schooner off the Coromandel coast had put his ship in dock for repairs. The *Tararua* had two officers: Robert Lindsay was chief officer and Edward Maloney second officer. Maloney held a second mate's certificate from Victoria and had been sailing round the New Zealand coast for 15 years. He had been with the Union Steam Ship Company for three and a half years and had not worked with Garrard before this posting. Robert Lindsay joined the U.S.S.Co. in November 1878, having previously been employed by McMeckan, Blackwood and Co. He had sailed on the coast for 20 years. Lindsay had worked with Garrard on their previous ship, the *Albion*, and transferred with him to the *Tararua*. At 29, Francis Garrard was the youngest ship's master in the Union Steam Ship Company, described as "dashing", "gallant" and "a young shipmaster of great promise" who was highly regarded by his employers for his "ability and attention to business".

Maloney took over the bridge from Garrard after they passed through the Heads and was relieved by Lindsay at 6pm when they were just south of Ocean Beach. The weather was fine and their speed 10 knots. They were steering by the land – the first course set for Nugget Point, then Slope Point, before setting a course west. Later a Melbourne newspaper described the coast the ship was passing for its readers: "For a considerable distance after leaving Dunedin the coastline trends in a south-westerly direction. The shore is bold, with deep water close to the strand. One of the principal landmarks is Nugget Point, a bold projecting headland with three pointed rocky islets nearly half a mile off. The lighthouse at the extremity of the point shows a fixed white light 250ft [76 metres] above the sea, which in clear weather can be seen about 20 miles [32 kilometres] off."[3]

The SS *Tararua*

The *Tararua* was one of the most comfortable steamboats on the Australia–New Zealand passenger-cargo route. It also had a reputation for punctuality. Shipping news was extensively covered in the papers and crew members of ships regularly calling at New Zealand ports often became well known figures. This lithograph was drawn by Albert Charles Cooke and was published in the *Illustrated New Zealand Herald* of 14 July 1881, two and a half months after the tragedy.

THE S.S. TARARUA WRECKED IN FOVEAUX STRAITS, 29TH APRIL, 1881.

ATL F-69980-1/2

Port Chalmers

A view of Port Chalmers in the 1880s showing both steam and sailing ships in the harbour. It was the home port for the *Tararua*.

Maloney took the bridge again at 8pm and was on duty until midnight when Lindsay returned. The night was very dark and clear overhead with a haze blanketing the land. Navigation now was by dead reckoning – using records of the vessel's speed, its last known position, and compass readings of the course they were steering. At 1.30am, about 10 minutes after he lost sight of the Nugget light, the first mate called Garrard to the bridge as instructed. They checked the distance travelled – 15 miles [24 kilometres] since 12 o'clock. According to Lindsay's estimates, that put them off Long Point. Darkness and haze made the land unreadable, but he estimated they were six to eight kilometres from the coast. Garrard set a new course, west-south-west, and left his first mate with instructions to call him at 3.45am. When he returned to the bridge, Lindsay placed their position as off Slope Point. Garrard instructed him to hold to his present course until the middle watch ended at 4am. When Maloney relieved Lindsay once more, the course was altered to west.

About 25 minutes after he came on duty, the second mate reported hearing breakers. Garrard ordered a change of course, to west by south, half south. Maloney held to it for about 25 minutes before it was altered back to west. At that time they checked the standard and forward compasses to ensure they tallied. Shortly after 5am the lookout changed and Charles Stewart relieved Frank Denz at the wheel while Denz went to get coffee. As he made for the stern to take the wheel, Stewart thought he saw Maloney on the bridge and the captain descending from it. The new lookout, able seaman John Weston, "saw the loom of the high land" and looking round saw the bridge was deserted, but someone at the stern. The bridge may well have been empty. About this time, Maloney left it to go back to Garrard again.

> "… When I went aft the second time, it was because I heard the sound of breakers," he explained. "It was very faint, and only a suspicion on my part. The lookout man was evidently awake and would turn about every half minute…. [The captain] was then looking at the chart on his table. He came and looked along on the starboard side and rushed to the steering wheel, which is aft in the Tararua…. He ordered the ship to be hauled off the shore…. He put the helm hard a-starboard. As the ship was coming round she struck…. I had seen nothing before she struck. After she struck, she dragged heavily for perhaps a few minutes and then bumped and settled down…. I saw the broken water around her. I could then see the head of the land."[4]

Garrard and Stewart had struggled with the wheel. "She answered her helm," said Stewart, "but I cannot say how far she came round. She struck immediately afterwards, about a minute after the captain rushed to the wheel. I stuck to the wheel until she broke the gear. She lifted the wheel up three times, and the gear all unshipped. I let go the wheel, and then caught hold of it again. I did not like to run away, so I stayed there a few seconds. Finding I could be of no further use, I went forward."[5] Meanwhile, Weston had been knocked from his feet. The lookout was on his way to the stern to check on the disturbed water. "I saw foam round the vessel and thought she was in some current. I did not sing out about it. I did not think the foam meant any danger. I saw nothing else and heard nothing before she struck. The foam was not like water breaking over rocks; it was boiling."[6]

Before Weston had regained his feet Garrard ordered the engines reversed, but to no effect – the propeller was broken and rudder unshipped when it struck.[7] He told Maloney to call all hands and clear away the lifeboats. Then he gave orders to stop the engines. The sound of breakers on shore was audible now through the mist and early morning gloom. Below decks, water was pouring into the vessel. Powerful waves pounded against the stern, pushing the ship forward and ripping away the rudder, wheel and after gear. Within minutes there was pandemonium. Husbands and wives travelling second class and accommodated in separate compartments now rushed to find each other, many still in their night clothes. William Hill, on his way to England, found his wife on deck, their small child clasped in her arms: "The vessel was bumping heavily on the rocks and a heavy sea was washing over her. I told my wife to hold on to a stanchion and went to see if there was any means of getting a boat. I found all was confusion."[8]

> "The passengers all came crowding up at once and for some minutes there was difficulty in controlling them," first mate Robert Lindsay remembered. He had woken with the jolt as the ship hit. There had been no lifeboat drill since taking over the Tararua and the crew had not been allocated specific lifeboat positions, so he went to the foremost boat. "While the boats were being cleared some passengers in their wish to get saved jumped into them before things were ready to swing them up to the davits. There was so much crowding that the men were hindered in getting the arrangements completed. The captain had to threaten to use force to keep them back, and it was with difficulty those who had got in were got out."[9]

Frank Denz had come back on deck with his coffee just as they hit. Married for two and a half years and with a 15-month-old daughter, he had persuaded his wife to bring the baby and come with him for a visit to Melbourne. He was immediately caught up in the chaos. "She was full of water almost at once. My wife, Mary Kelly and another woman who was naked clung to me. The back waters of the sea that broke over the ship carried us right aft. The women all screamed at first but were soon brave and believed us when we said that there was no danger. They were put in the smoking house and covered. I put a rug and my jacket on my wife. I was not more afraid than the rest, but the wife

A fatal Point

Waipapa Point was one of the most notorious spots on a dangerous coast. Sandhills form a low lying coastline and the sandy beach quickly turns to a rocky sea bed. There is a heavy ground swell even on fine days, but 24 hours of south-easterly winds had built up a very heavy sea when the *Tararua* was caught on Otara Reef.

THE WRECK OF THE STEAMSHIP TARARUA ON THE WAIPAPA REEF, FOVEAUX STRAITS.

kept clinging to me and that made me weak. The captain was cross and scolded me, but I could not push her out at such a time."[10]

Gradually order was established. It took 20 minutes to make the five lifeboats ready but Garrard delayed launching until daybreak after the first attempt had failed: as the starboard boat was being lowered from the davits, the sea struck and it was holed. While they waited, the signal cannons were fired five or six times and distress rockets launched. When dawn broke shortly after six on Friday morning, they could see where they were for the first time. The *Tararua* had run aground on Otara Reef, north of Slope Point and just under a kilometre from shore. The reef extends nearly 13 kilometres out to sea from Waipapa Point at the north-east extremity of Foveaux Strait.

The second lifeboat was launched some time before six o'clock, with Maloney, four crew and a passenger, George Lawrence.[11] Garrard had called for strong swimmers.

> **"The captain asked me if I could swim and if I would go in the boat and see if I could get to land,"** Lawrence said. **"When [we] were about 500 yards from the ship and about the same distance from the shore, the mate told me to stand by and he would give me a chance to go ashore in a lull. I jumped and struggled until I was in the surf, which was so heavy that I rolled over many times. I kept my senses and at last got in on the top of a breaker. I was cold, so I ran about the beach to circulate the blood. When warm, I made for a house about half a mile off…."**[12]

The farm workers at Charles and Frederick Brunton's Otara station were preparing for work when an exhausted Lawrence appeared at the door of one of the station huts asking for help. He was carrying a message from Garrard. One of the hands, Charles Gilbee,[13] rode first to Fortrose where he informed the postmaster and then on to the nearest telegraph office at Wyndham. He rode fast, covering the 53 kilometres before midday. The first message went to Dunedin to James Mills, the managing director of the shipping company: "12.15pm 29 April 81…. SS *Tararua* on Otara reef. Assistance wanted." It was not marked urgent and was the second message about the *Tararua* Mills had received that morning. The company's agents in Bluff had telegraphed asking when the vessel had left Port Chalmers, as it had not yet arrived. Mills had not been concerned: the area's weather could sometimes delay a ship up to 24 hours. Now he telegraphed back to Wyndham urgently: "*Hawea* leaves this afternoon. Send word to *Tararua*. Is *Tararua* in danger." News of the stranding was telegraphed to Invercargill: "The SS *Tararua* due at Bluff this morning from the north struck at Otara Reef near Toi Tois this morning. All lives are safe at present the vessel is close inshore." This was the cable printed in some Friday newspapers.

But the information guiding the rescuers had almost nothing in common with the situation at the wreck. Only 10 minutes after Charles Gilbee rode off, the first people died. Maloney's lifeboat had gone back to the ship and six more passengers who thought they could reach the shore through the breakers were lowered from the yard arm. Lawrence got back to the beach just in time to help three of them from the surf.

SHIPWRECK

The other three failed to make it. The sea, which had been comparatively smooth until 9am, now began to roughen with the incoming tide and a rising wind. Meanwhile, the ship's owners responded casually to offers of help: "Not absolutely necessary for *Kakanui* to call but can do so if not out of her way and offer assistance. Also inform captain of *Tararua* the *Hawea* will be with him at daylight."[14]

On the ship, the chief cook was below deck in the galley. Antonio Miscellief[15] came originally from Malta and had been at sea for many years. This trip on the *Tararua* was to be his last before leaving the sea to start a business in Dunedin with the chief steward, Charles Ellen. He had already been through one shipwreck on the West Coast. After the ship struck the reef, Miscellief, who had been up on deck at the time, first took care of the chief engineer's son until his mother took him. Then he helped move passengers from the saloon forward to the smoking cabin because the sea was breaking up the back of the vessel. When the tide was well down, Garrard asked him to go below and prepare a substantial meal for everyone. He worked until the galley flooded.

The reef itself became the focus of hope for those on the ship and on shore. George Lawrence fought his way through the surf again and swam out to try and get a line ashore there to help land passengers, but he found it impossible. He was washed off and managed to make it back to the beach. On the *Tararua*, William Hill had been surveying the shore and noticed a smooth part near the reef. He asked Garrard if there was any possibility of landing there. The captain sent the surf boat to check. "When she came back the carpenter said he thought it was possible to land on the reef. A kedge anchor was put in the boat. I asked the captain to allow me to go to the reef and examine it,"[16] Hill recounted. He did not tell Garrard that he had 10 years' service at sea before coming ashore 15 years earlier. "I can swim," Hill explained.

> "He said, 'Will you do so?' I said I would and I would hold up my hat if it was prudent. He replied, 'Not only your hat but your hands.'… One of the firemen went with me, and the boat's crew. On nearing the reef in the second mate's boat, we found it was not so smooth as it appeared. It was very rough and there was a heavy sea rolling over it. The fireman swam from the boat to the surf. It was a very dangerous place…. The second mate asked me if I would land. I said, 'No.'"[17]

When he left his wife and child in the smoking room with the other women and children, William Hill knew he would not be allowed to stay with them. He told his wife that if there was a chance of helping to get assistance, he would do it. Before he went with Maloney, he arranged with Garrard to send the women first if it was safe to land on the reef. But he saw there was no chance of that. Maloney took him back to the stranded vessel to tell the captain and take aboard three more passengers who said they could swim to shore. The boat then returned to the reef. Fireman James Maher had tried to reach the beach only a few metres away from where they had left him, but could not get through the floating kelp. Once they were reasonably close in, the three passengers jumped into the waves and struck out for land. It took all the fireman's strength to make it back to the lifeboat. He was pulled on board battered and exhausted. Then Maloney discovered that they could no longer get alongside the *Tararua*. The waves were growing bigger and wilder. The lifeboat was caught and nearly capsized. The three swimmers had disappeared, consumed by the sea. Those stranded on the ship watched the attrition with mounting fear and horror. The women begged the captain not to make them leave.

Meanwhile, the first mate had been put in charge of the surf boat. The carpenter had been ordered to let Lindsay take over, and relinquished his seat with relief. Many, including Garrard, believed the ship was the best place to be. As Lindsay prepared to leave, the Rev. J.B. Richardson, one of a number of Wesleyan clergy travelling to Australia for a church conference, wished him luck and said quietly, "Have confidence in yourself and take the boat away safely." The first mate noted that the captain was "perfectly cool and calm". Frank Denz had also been ordered into the boat, to replace another sailor who, the crew complained, was too busy avoiding getting wet to row properly. The man climbed back on board, also pleased to be out of it. The last thing Denz wanted was to replace him.

> "I was crying as I could not bear leaving the wife and child. The captain was not cross then. He persuaded me and held out his arms for the child. I gave her to him and said, 'Now, my captain, you'll look after her won't you?' He said, 'Yes, Frank, I will; be sure of that.'"[18]

While Maloney, Hill and the others stood off from the *Tararua*, Lindsay, Denz, John Weston and two other crew, three passengers and a young boy set out first for the reef and then the beach. They carried heaving lines. Lindsay planned to have one of them jump out of the boat and take one line ashore. They would then tie the other lines to the end of it. But just before they reached the breakers, a "blind roller" caught the 7.3-metre boat and they capsized: "[I]t upset end over end and not sideways," Denz said. "That will show you how rough the sea was. We all got ashore but the boy who cleaned the brass on the ship. Just before we upset the poor little chap said, 'I believe it's through me the vessel struck, for I am very unlucky.' I dare say those on board thought it very hard that we did not come back, but they saw the fix we were in. I would have gone back for the wife [even] if I had been sure of being lost."

The surf boat had split open at both ends and all attempts to repair it well enough to relaunch it into the increasingly violent waves were useless. They looked out across the glittering broken water to the broken ship under the bright midday sun. On board, Garrard was still of the opinion that the safest place for the remaining passengers was the ship and that it would hold together until their rescuers arrived. Those who had left it were now positive that not even a boat much larger than theirs could get close enough to help. Maloney had tried repeatedly and failed. One of his crew was thrown from the boat during an attempt but managed to climb in again. Nothing now could be done and he pulled

THE WRECK OF THE TARARUA.—LAWRENCE'S SWIM THROUGH THE BREAKERS.

Swimming through the breakers

When Captain Garrard called for strong swimmers, passenger George Lawrence responded. He managed to reach shore and ran for help, but he was one of the very few to make it to land alive.

The *Tararua*'s mail

The *Tararua* was carrying a mail consignment when it went down. These letters are from the eight that were later recovered from the wreck.

Robin Gwynn

back a distance from the ship to keep clear of the reef. The only doctor on board, Dr Donald Campbell, was kept busy. Charles Ellen had severed a finger getting out stores to feed the passengers. One of the bedroom stewards had broken his leg. Campbell set it and he was carried up to the forecastle and laid on a mattress. An hour or so later he was washed overboard in a heavy sea. Lindsay, watching helplessly from the beach, said those on board appeared to be calm, "as if they were prepared to meet any fate that might befall them".[19] Frank Denz kept a fierce watch on his baby, still in the captain's arms.

The men who had made it to shore built a fire and began going up to the farm in twos and threes to get dry clothes and food. By late morning, the first people had arrived to help. They brought food and blankets expecting to find all the passengers on shore and in need of warmth and supplies. Miners from the area also arrived and helped build up the fire. Later they described the experience to reporters: "Those on the beach were… rendered powerless to assist. Could anything have been done, it would have been attempted…. Those who were there say they often wished to leave but were bound to the spot by a species of fascination.… They could only look on in sickening suspense."[20] They would stay now, through the afternoon and night and into the following day.

As more and more of the stern sank beneath the waves, the passengers were moved forward – men, women and children into the forecastle and the crew up into the rigging. Antonio Miscellief recalled:

> "About 2pm on Friday, the ship was fast breaking up and had driven further in shore. The captain then gave orders to carry the females to the forecastle head. He carried some himself, from the smoking room to the bridge, and we took them forward. We afterwards got on the forecastle and the captain said, 'I have done all I can. I have no boats available. The tide will be out in another half hour, and I will try to do the best I can.' Immediately he ended speaking, a heavy sea came and carried away the dinghy and the cutter."[21]

They were the last of the boats on board. The sky had clouded over and the afternoon "turned dreary". Now the sea began to pick them off one by one, catching up and sweeping people over the side. Maloney and his crew struggled to get their boat into a position to save them, but each time the high seas defeated them. On the steamer, Miscellief described a scene of bravery and desperation. Dr Campbell continued to work and was trying to splint an engineer's broken leg. A small boy who he thought was one of the doctor's five children had his arms spread wide trying to stop his smaller sisters from sliding down the deck and off to leeward. Women and children were huddled together in the bows crying. The purser was kissing and consoling his wife, telling her if things came to the worst they must be brave. The rear of the steamer was under water now as far as the mainmast with only her forecastle head projecting above. Another heavy sea struck the ship and as passengers rushed to the side away from it, the railing gave way and about 18 or 20 of them, including Dr Campbell, the engineer, the purser and his wife, Mary Kelly and the cook, were swept into the sea. Miscellief heard Garrard cry out, "Oh God, what are we to do now?"

The cook caught hold of Mary Kelly, shouting to those on board to throw him a rope. The men in the rigging hung frozen and silent. After struggling to keep them both afloat for several minutes, another powerful wave pulled the young woman from his grasp and she disappeared from sight. Miscellief struck out for the shore. The water was full of floating wreckage but he got clear of it. When he reached the beach he was taken to the farm, given dry clothes and put to bed for a while. Miscellief was the only one of the many who set out from the ship to swim to shore who reached it and lived. Again and again that afternoon, those on the beach saw people clinging to wreckage trying to make their way to land. But they lost their hold and sank below the waves or were sucked out to sea again, sometimes only metres from safety.

By late afternoon when the *Tararua* split apart amidships, all the women and children had fallen or been washed into the sea. The men who remained were clustered in the rigging. On shore, Denz believed he could still see his child in the captain's arms: "I kept my eye on them as it grew dark. The last thing I saw was the captain holding my little girl."[22] Maloney turned his boat to stand further out to sea in the hope of meeting up with a passing vessel and getting help. Back at the *Tararua*'s home port, the *Hawea* was finally ready to set out at 5pm, a full 12 hours after the steamer hit the reef. It carried food to feed all the passengers for several days and heavy cables to pull a stranded ship off the rocks. On the way down harbour, they slowed to tow a sailing schooner out to open sea.[23] The *Kakanui* had left Bluff an hour before, its sailing delayed until high tide. It would be many hours yet before either reached Waipapa Point.

A second night closed on the wreck. The beach bonfire was built higher while matches glimmered intermittently like fireflies among the men still clinging and lashed to the rigging. Some time after midnight, a cheer echoed across the water. Ship's lights, possibly the *Kakanui*, had been sighted, but rescue was impossible – still no ship or boat could get close enough to what was left of the *Tararua*. At about 2.30am, a man's voice, probably Garrard's, was heard above the breakers, shouting in desperation for someone to send a boat. Those on the beach could hear screams. The end when it came was sudden and loud. There was a great crash and then silence. The masts had broken and the hull rolled over onto its side. At first light the steamer had sunk almost out of sight and wreckage, cargo, mailbags and the occasional body littered the surface of the sea.

The *Prince Rupert* was already standing by. After 20 hours in the lifeboat, Maloney and those with him had met up with the schooner at 2.30 on Saturday morning. Between 6am and 7am, the *Kakanui* and *Hawea* came abreast of the point. The *Kakanui* had seen the bonfire some distance away and believed all was well. Now those on the three vessels surveyed the devastation around them. As Maloney joined James Mills on the *Hawea* to describe the last 24 hours, people were opening their Saturday morning newspapers to the comforting news that the steamer's passengers and crew were all safely ashore. The first newspaper reporters, arriving later that day, found instead 20 cold survivors, chilled helpers and just the points of the *Tararua*'s

Coins from the wreck

These coins were also recovered from the wreck. Several thousand pounds worth of old coins were being returned to England for re-minting. They have deteriorated further in the rough seas.

Robin Gwynn

bowsprit and mizzen-mast sticking out above the surf. For several hours the *Hawea* searched the area for anyone still alive, but with no success.

Daylight also began the awful task of recovering what bodies could be found. One of the first was a badly bruised baby, picked up by a boat from the *Hawea*. When they called William Hill to see if he could identify her, he collapsed on the deck – it was his little daughter. Lindsay, Maloney and local settlers began retrieving bodies as they found them along the beach. Most were naked or semi-naked and often badly cut and disfigured by rocks and wreckage. As the days passed, the decomposing bodies washed ashore were no longer recognisable. The coroner instructed them to be buried immediately. The gruesome job took its toll on the police recovery team and those who came to help. Some like James Wybrow, a local and a strong swimmer who helped retrieve bodies entangled in the kelp, had terrible nightmares for months afterwards.[24]

The number of bodies washing ashore in such a remote and undeveloped area soon became a problem. The first of them, 10 adults and a child, were buried in the cemetery at Fortrose. However, it quickly became apparent the small cemetery could not take so many bodies, and was too far away. The tracks and roads between Wyndham and the beach had broken up so badly with the amount of traffic in the two weeks following the wreck that it became difficult to make the return journey in a day. Tararua Acre, a patch of land behind the sandhills at Otara almost opposite the site of the wreck, was set aside for a special cemetery. Fifty-five more bodies were finally buried there. Captain Garrard's body, wrapped in kelp, was found washed ashore on 10 May. He was buried initially at Otara until his family arranged for his re-burial in Barbadoes Street Cemetery, Christchurch. Of the 131 passengers and crew who died in the wreck, some 74 were recovered before the police beach patrol was withdrawn. Of the 20 who survived, 12 were crew and eight were passengers, all from second class.

A Court of Nautical Assessors was convened on Tuesday 10 May in Dunedin to inquire into the loss of the *Tararua*. The passenger steamer had run foul of one of the most notorious spots on the New Zealand coast. Waipapa Point is at the eastern entrance to Foveaux Strait and more lives have been lost in shipwrecks there than anywhere else in New Zealand. In addition to the low lie of the land, the mists that often obscure it even in fine weather, and strong currents which drag ships towards the shore, the coastline itself was mapped incorrectly on some charts. Nevertheless, well before the hearing began some newspaper editorials were placing the blame with the captain. They reminded readers that as well as being only 29 he had already been involved in three shipwrecks, two in positions of command: as acting chief officer and as captain. Yet no one had died and he had been exonerated of any wrong-doing on both those occasions. His family engaged a lawyer to represent his interests at the inquiry.

Early in the hearings it emerged that Garrard had revised his high opinion of his first mate. After arguments about admitting this into evidence, one of the assessors requested it be discussed as "he could not think of a first officer reduced to a mere automaton, as [Lindsay] was in this case".[25] James Mills said on the stand he had received a telegram from the captain asking for a change of chief officer when he reached Port Chalmers.

"When the ship arrived I had a conversation with Captain Garrard, the result of which was that it was agreed that, if he wished it, the change would be made at once, but as our spare chief officer was not on the spot, we preferred to postpone the change until Captain Garrard's return from Melbourne. He was satisfied with that arrangement. Apart from the merits of the case, we would make the change at the request of a master. We could not have a master and mate on such terms."[26]

During the course of giving evidence, it became very clear from the mate's testimony that his relations with the captain were extremely strained. Soon after this, the lawyer representing Robert Lindsay and Edward Maloney demanded to know the exact powers of the court and whether the two officers were to be charged; and if so, with what they would be charged. The court said it was considering whether there had been "some wrongful act or default on the part of officers which caused the wreck".

The Court of Inquiry returned the certificates of the first and second mates. It found the primary cause of the wreck and loss of life was "the failure of the master, Francis George Garrard, to ascertain at 4am on the 29th April the correct position of the ship. The simple use of the lead [a heavy lead ball on the end of a rope lowered over the side to test the depth of the water] would have told the distance off shore."[27] The immediate cause of the wreck was "the negligent failure of the able seaman, Weston, to keep a proper lookout, for we are impressed with the idea that had a proper lookout been kept the broken water must have been observed some minutes before the vessel struck, and in all probability sufficient time afforded for the danger to be avoided".[28] The court also recommended that the government set up a lighthouse near the point and that all passenger vessels in New Zealand waters should carry lifebelts for the maximum number of passengers and crew. (The *Tararua* was allowed to carry 224 passengers and had five lifeboats that could take 165 people in total, plus six lifebuoys and 12 lifebelts.)

Despite the scale of the disaster, the first light did not shine on the point until New Year's Day 1884. Long before that, attempts were under way to recover the sunken bullion. Within two weeks of the disaster, the government had commissioned a salvage operation. It ended without success and after losing anchors, buoys and even a surf boat in the rough seas. Another attempt by divers in 1889 lasted for more than five months but the weather and sea conditions defeated them. A diver who followed immediately after was no luckier. It was 1970 before divers salvaged something of value – over $8000 worth of brass and copper fittings and ship's souvenirs. But the salvage was illegal as the wreck was privately owned by then by Joan MacIntosh, author of a book on the *Tararua*. Despite her best efforts to control the site, the pirating continued. Eventually diver Kelly Tarlton bought the wreck from her, intending to recover the silver; but a mistake in setting explosives to break up the concretion scattered debris so wide that no trace of the "treasure" was found.

The Last on the Wreck

Another dramatic sketch from the *Illustrated New Zealand Herald*. The caption reads: "They were washed away one by one, til at last only one man with a child in his arms remained." Chief Officer Lindsay said he could not see anyone holding a child as night fell, but Frank Denz believed the captain carried his baby daughter until the end.

BLACK SUNDAY —
The Wreck of the
BEN VENUE

For many years, the port at Timaru had a reputation as a ships' graveyard: between 1866 and 1886, 21 ships were wrecked in and around Timaru harbour. But loss of the *City of Cashmere* on Ninety Mile Beach north of the Timaru lighthouse in January 1882 began its worst year — in just over four months four large vessels went ashore and nine men lost their lives.

There had been criticism of the harbour as a port almost since the first sailing ship moored there in 1852. In 1856, the Canterbury Association agent Henry Sewell dismissed it as "a miserable apology for a shipping place, without wood or water. Nothing will ever spring up there but a public house, a store and a woolshed".[1] A month after the *City of Cashmere* was wrecked, the Australasian Insurance and Banking Record remarked: "The natural desire of the people of Timaru to have a harbour of their own has led them to induce ship after ship to its destruction."[2] It thought the borough's wish to be independent of Christchurch was laudable, but questioned the wisdom of wasting money on such a patently unsuitable harbour.

That desire for independence had been an issue in the region for 20 years, as had sometimes bitter inter-port rivalry. Prestige, land values, government development money and farming costs were all affected by the success a community had in encouraging shipping to call at the local port. Timaru was in competition with several harbours down the South Island's east coast, including Oamaru, Port Chalmers and Lyttelton.

The Ben Venue

Type: iron full-rigged ship
Built: Messrs Barclay, Curle and Co, Glasgow, Scotland, 1867
Length: 64 metres (210 feet)
Beam: 10.7 metres (35 feet 1 inch)
Depth: 6.3 metres (20 feet 7 inches)
Tonnage: 999 tons register
Port of registry: Glasgow
Owner: Messrs Watson Brothers, Glasgow
Master: Captain William G. McGowan
Cargo: approx. 500 tons coal
Destined voyage: London via Port Chalmers
Date of wreck: 14 May 1882
Location of wreck: Caroline Bay, Timaru
Lives lost: nine — three from the *City of Perth* and six from Timaru

The *Ben Venue*

The "Home" ship moored in calm waters. It was one of four large vessels wrecked in Timaru Harbour early in 1882.

Timaru was not a natural harbour. It had two principal disadvantages: it was exposed to storms from the south-east that drove ships towards the shore; and had a harbour bottom of hard basalt rock covered with only a thin layer of sand. This meant there was no secure anchorage to hold vessels in difficult weather conditions. Since the end of the 1850s, the growing community had discussed ways to give visiting ships some protection. Meanwhile trade vessels dropped anchor offshore while smaller whale boats and surf boats ferried cargo and passengers to and from the landing sheds on the beach. There was a regular and ongoing battle between the ships' captains and the owners of the landing services over how far in the big vessels should be moored. The landing service wanted the ships as close to the beach as possible to make it easy and quick to load and unload. The vessels' masters preferred to stay further out. It was well known that the main cause of wrecking and stranding was the south-eastern swells and storms which drove ships onshore.

By 1882, Captain Alexander Mills had been the harbour master at Timaru for 14 years. Scottish by birth, he had come to New Zealand after sailing the world. For two years he was the pilot at Bluff and then sailed as first officer on the SS *Albion* until he was appointed to take charge of the Government Landing Service at Timaru as harbour master. Two years after he arrived, a breakwater just over two metres high and 26 metres long was built out to the reef next to the landing service. But it proved no match for the sea and was swept away. In 1878, construction began on a second, concrete breakwater, but only after several years of in-fighting among members of the recently established harbour board. The endless arguments and resultant inaction of both the board and borough council were criticised at the time, and by later commentators.[3] The events of 1882 were a good example of this friction and its effect.

The stranding and then total wreck of the *City of Cashmere* at the beginning of the year was significant in that it was the first "Home" vessel lost at Timaru. The ship drifted sedately ashore on a fine, windless, Sunday afternoon in moderate seas after an anchor cable parted when a bolt worked loose from a shackle. Unsuccessful attempts had been made to tow it out to sea before it grounded. Captain Mills and the vessel's crew eventually had to be taken off by the port's emergency service, the Timaru Volunteer Rocket Brigade, in the early hours of the morning. All chance of refloating the ship was lost when it turned broadside on to the breakers after daybreak and was washed up high on the beach.

> As the *Timaru Herald* pointed out, although this time the wreck was not caused by "the perils of the Timaru roadstead... for all that, the disaster can hardly fail to do Timaru a great deal of harm. Those who are interested in decrying the port will of course make the very worst of it".[4]

The need for a powerful steam tug to tow ships in such situations from danger was canvassed again, and the harbour board urged to get on with the breakwater's construction and put aside "obstinacy and perversity".[5] The great concern with the loss of a "Home" ship on the Britain–New Zealand run was that overseas shipping companies might stop calling at Timaru, or that insurance rates for the port would increase.

Tensions and conflicting interests continued, however. In April, the harbour board received a letter of complaint from the captains of four ships in harbour about the "entire inadequacy of loading and discharging facilities".[6] There were fewer whale and surf boats available to shift cargo and passengers, even though the board was trying to build up business in the port. The board's secretary, W.J. Tennent, was unsympathetic, replying that any problems were partly of the masters' own making. But the issue was raised again when on 2 May the fully laden wooden barque *Duke of Sutherland* bumped on the harbour bottom in heavy seas, sank in Caroline Bay and was totally wrecked the next day. It had been moored 1.2 kilometres from shore, Captain Mills having refused to bring it any closer in. The harbour master constantly warned big ships against anchoring too close inshore whereas the harbour board placed heavy pressure on captains to bring their vessels farther in than they wanted to, sometimes refusing landing services unless they did.

Mills spent long hours on the disabled vessel, at times with only its master to assist, trying to save the *Duke of Sutherland*. When that proved impossible, he organised for it to be towed clear of the anchorage area before the ship was left to drift to shore and break up. There was now a second "Home" vessel lost and, like the *City of Cashmere*, just as it was ready to sail. But the *Duke of Sutherland* had been kept waiting at anchor for weeks with repeated delays in loading because of lack of working appliances, despite complaints

Captain Alexander Mills
The harbour master was well thought of in Timaru but had enemies on the harbour board. He was given notice and his job advertised. He was only re-appointed after two moves to employ other men were defeated. Three days later, the Timaru Roadstead had its worst shipping disaster.

to Tennent and the harbour board. At the inquiry that followed, a number of people said the ship's hull and frame were worm-eaten and rotten and it was decided the ship's unseaworthiness was the cause of the wreck. Later reports completely refuted those statements, one more instance of conflicting and contradictory claims shifting blame.

At the time of the wreck, Mills' job was under threat. A couple of weeks earlier, the board had given him notice and called for applications for his position. At the end of a heated board meeting on 11 May, Alexander Mills was reappointed harbour master at Timaru. Three days later the port with a suspect reputation had its worst shipping catastrophe.

People in the district waking during the first hours of Sunday 14 May heard a sound last heard on a Sunday in September 1878, the day four ships in port were wrecked. The low rumble and roar of surf on the shore could be heard many kilometres from the harbour. There were five vessels in port at the time – a Norwegian barque, *C.F. Funch*, anchored at the ballast grounds just over three kilometres out, two "Home" ships moored about 800 metres from the breakwater at the inner anchorage, the *Ben Venue* and *City of Perth*, and two schooners, *Kate McGregor* and *Julius Vogel*, lying inside the breakwater. The harbour master, concerned about weather conditions, had been on watch all night. There was no wind but from about 12 o'clock on Saturday night the seas began to rise from the south-east and increase in force without warning. High tide was at 1am and once it began to ebb the waves became more violent.

"[Captain McGowan of the *Ben Venue*, nicknamed 'Mad McGowan'[7]] states that about one o'clock on Sunday morning the sea became very heavy and the vessel, which was lying stern to it, began to roll and lurch heavily. Several blind rollers came on board, breaking in some of the stern windows and sweeping the poop. All hands were then called and soon afterwards a very heavy sea struck her and it was thought she had hit the ground, but on examination it was discovered her rudder had been broken and the rest of her stern ports smashed."[8]

A short distance away the *City of Perth* was also riding rough, as Captain Colin McDonald recalled:

> "About two o'clock in the morning, while stern on, the sea broke in the cabin windows. The force of the sea was so great that I was afraid the stern would be beaten in. Towards daylight I got all hands on deck and put two men at the wheel. I then noticed she was riding head to the sea, and dragging down towards the ship Benvenue [sic]. I let go the port anchor and paid out cable on the starboard one and put on a spring. After a while I let go the patent anchor with a hawser attached as I was afraid the vessel would go on top of the Benvenue...."[9]

The crew got the boats ready to lower.

At first light Mills could see the two "Home" ships at the inner anchorage were "riding heavily" and fired the lighthouse's signal gun for the rocket brigade to assemble on the foreshore. The brigade kept watch during storms and helped take crews off ships

CITY OF PERTH AND BEN VENUE IN CAROLINE BAY. TIMARU. 1882 J. DICKIE.

"A ship's graveyard"

On a sunny Sunday afternoon in 1882, one ship and nine lives were lost. Crowds gathered to watch the *Ben Venue* and the *City of Perth* run aground under the cliffs at the Timaru Roadstead. By the turn of the century, an extended breakwater, two wharves and the north mole at last provided a safe anchorage.

Life savers

Some of the crew of the rocket brigade's lifeboat *Alexandra*. From left: G. Shirtcliffe, C.G. Vogeler, A.H. Turnbull and A.L. Haycock. They are wearing medals presented to them by St. John's Masonic Lodge for their heroic efforts on "Black Sunday".

in trouble by firing their two Boxers "rocket" guns out to the vessel with ropes attached to mortar shells. The crews were then helped ashore by breeches buoy – a pair of canvas trousers on a rope used for rescuing people. Mills sent the brigade to the cliffs at the south end of the Waimataitai Lagoon in case the barque *C.F. Funch* broke its cables and was driven in that direction.

At sun-up, all five vessels were still at anchor but there was an extremely heavy sea running and the white tops of broken rollers were visible for several kilometres out to sea. Overhead there was a clear sky, bright sun, and no wind. The two schooners inside the breakwater and the barque out at the ballast grounds were handling the seas well, but the other two did not look safe. The *Ben Venue* had put out another anchor but had also become destabilised when it dropped into the trough of a wave and the coal in its hold was thrown over to starboard. The ship now had a heavy list. By 8.30am it was flying a distress signal and one of its cables had parted, but shortly after 9am there was a change in weather conditions that offered a chance to escape from what was rapidly becoming a dangerous situation.

A breeze sprang up from the north-west and the sea looked as if it was quieting. The *Ben Venue* slowly swung round with its bow to land; the foretopsail on the *City of Perth* was loosened. Captain Mills ran up a variety of signals, including one to the *Ben Venue* telling them to trim their cargo – they had tried repeatedly, but every time the coal was shovelled away, the ship would roll and throw it back to starboard. He signalled all vessels to make ready to put to sea. The wind was light and variable. The *Ben Venue* ran up the signal "Sailing" and as it was loaded and ready to leave for Port Chalmers, Mills presumed it would raise anchors as soon as it was stable again. Mills then signalled *City of Perth*, now also swinging round to face north-west, asking if anything was wrong. The vessel answered "All right" and the rocket brigade and harbour master began to think the emergency over. Then, much to the brigade's surprise, the *Ben Venue* signalled that it was drifting and wanted an anchor. As far as Mills was concerned, it was too rough to send out a boat. Up along the cliffs and breakwater and on the foreshore, a sizeable crowd began to gather.

On the *City of Perth*, Captain McDonald ordered the mainsail and foresail set. Then, as quickly as the wind had come up, it died away. The vessel continued to swing round, and, to stop the anchor cables becoming entangled, McDonald ordered the port anchor raised. But when they pulled it up they found it already fouled with the starboard chain. As the crew worked to free it, the ship pitched and rolled. "I was going to clear the anchor, when a heavy sea struck the ship and tore it away, the cable having parted before," the ship's boatswain John Lynch said later. "When the preventer went, it broke one of the chief officer's legs. The ship then again swung head to sea. About an hour afterwards, the starboard chain parted."

The *Ben Venue* was also having problems with its anchors and cables. "About 12.30pm, the third anchor was all ready, but owing to the lurching of the vessel, the task of getting it over the side was attended with difficulty and danger," Captain McGowan afterwards reported. "Shortly before one o'clock the second anchor parted, and as it was found the ship was drifting, and gradually settling over, the crew who were below trimming the cargo at the time were called on deck and got into one of the boats. The vessel… was stuck to until she got into broken water…"[10]

The rocket brigade were monitoring the deteriorating situation and set up their equipment on the cliffs near Woollcombe's Lagoon ready to rescue the ship's crew. But as they waited, the boat with the crew was lowered and headed for the *City of Perth* where the men were taken on board. However, any relief among the watchers on shore was short-lived. The crowd had been transfixed by the *Ben Venue*'s drift to destruction. "Very steadily and very quietly did the doomed ship drift towards the shore, and had she been sailing into a dock and under a careful steersman, she could not have headed straighter for her goal. She was within 50 yards [45 metres] of the beach before she struck the ground, and when she did so, she gradually canted broadside on to the sea, and was soon almost high and dry…."[11]

When attention returned to the *City of Perth* they saw that it was also adrift, flying its ensign upside down – a sign of distress – and a signal requesting "medical assistance". With the starboard chain broken, the only thing holding the ship now was the hawser which, according to McDonald, was already badly chafed:

> "I ordered the lifeboat and another to be got ready and prepared to leave the ship as I was afraid to stop by her. Before leaving I went forward twice to inspect the hawser which I saw could not long hold her. For the safety of life we abandoned the vessel about 2.15pm…. There were 26 of us in all in two boats. We got ashore alright after great difficulty."[12]

The crew and lifeboat from the *Ben Venue* came with them together with a boat with a volunteer crew that had gone out to see if they could give any help. As the crew was helped up the wharf steps, they warned that only a stout hawser was now holding the *City of Perth*. It could be seen "standing out at times taut and rigid as an iron rod".[13]

At this point, the rocket brigade and the hundreds of locals watching the drama, and the two ships' crews, now safely ashore, believed there was little more to come, except the probable stranding of the *City of Perth* if the last cable failed to hold. Even though the sea had gone down slightly, it seemed unlikely the worn hawser could take the heavy strain. McDonald had gone to telephone the ship's agent in Christchurch when he was told that "a boat's crew was being picked up quietly"[14] to take the harbour master out to his ship. McDonald was stunned. He had only reached land 12 to 15 minutes earlier. Without even finishing the phone call, he ran down to the landing steps. "Captain Mills was in a boat a little way off, the men lying on their oars, they had not pulled off then," he told an inquiry into the incident. "I stood on the top of the steps and called to them to come and take me, but I cannot say whether they heard me or not, or whether they made any sign. They could scarcely help hearing me. My own lifeboat was lying close to them when I hailed and the men in it heard me. But there was a crowd on the wharf at the time...."[15]

McDonald, mistrustful of Mill's intentions, got into his gig, the second mate insisting on coming with him, and rowed hard in pursuit. When the ship's carpenter in charge of the *City of Perth* lifeboat saw the captain heading for their ship, he set off as well with seven other members of the crew. Three boats and 23 men were making their way through difficult seas to a ship only just abandoned.

Mills' decision to go out to a vessel its master had felt compelled to quit set in motion a sequence which culminated in tragedy. Later Captain Sutter, Mayor of Timaru and an ex officio member of the harbour board, claimed angrily that, "If the first boat had not gone, neither would the second or the third."[16] Although Sutter and some other board members were once again trying to deflect culpability from the board's landing services, it is certain that if Mills had not gone, no one else would have either. But Mills was in an invidious position. Under law, the harbour master/pilot is responsible for the safety of ships in his harbour, not the ship's master. He had just won back his job with great difficulty a few days earlier. His judgement on where large vessels could be safely moored had been repeatedly questioned and sometimes overridden. Earlier that year he had been publicly accused by his employers of lack of nerve and courage. And finally, he had been on watch all night anticipating just such a scenario and so had not slept. Mills' decision was to prove fatal for him and eight other men.

The first person Mills told of his decision to go out to the ship was William Collis, a diver and the harbour board's coxswain. Collis met up with him as Mills returned from checking the rocket brigade at the lighthouse station and the *Ben Venue*.

> "He said, 'Bill, they have all deserted the *City of Perth*. We must try and save her if possible.' I replied, 'It is our duty to try and do so.' ... I got a crew and we went down and launched the whaleboat. Before we went afloat, Captain Mills told Hamilton to go up to the Captain of the *City of Perth* with his compliments, and tell him he was going off to try and save the vessel 'with no bad intention'. I understood from this that Captain Mills meant he was simply going to do his duty."[17]

Unfortunately, it seems McDonald never received the message.

Before Mills had set out, those watching from shore could see that a breeze from the south was filling the topsail of the *City of Perth*. As soon as Mills was on board he ordered the sail rolled up. Captain McDonald arrived only minutes later, and some time after, the carpenter's lifeboat. When the captain was questioned later about what had taken place on board, it became apparent he feared Mills had gone to claim salvage rights to the vessel.

McDonald went up and asked the harbour master what he intended to do. Mills told him he was trying to save the ship "without any bad intention" and asked if there was a kedge anchor on deck as he wanted to try putting one out. McDonald showed him the frayed hawser, warning it was unlikely to hold even half an hour, and then said, "You have not enough men to handle [the kedge]. You don't expect to work my ship with four or five men when I had to leave her with twenty-six?"[18] At this point, the worn cable holding the ship finally parted. On shore a shout went up – "She's gone!" Although Collis said it had been Mills' intention to come ashore with the vessel, the arrival of the two other boats changed that. When McDonald said they would all have to leave, there was no argument. Perhaps to ensure everyone did leave, he went with Mills in the whaleboat.

The three boats set out for shore through huge rollers and were soon in trouble. As they fought their way through enormous waves, the *City of Perth* drifted gradually towards the beach until it came to rest upright, its stern against the *Ben Venue*. The brilliant sunshine gave the unfolding drama a fierce illumination. The first two boats had almost got inside the breakwater when the third, which was well back and being driven to the north, was caught on top of an enormous wave and overturned. Both the other boats immediately turned back, Mills instructing his crew to strip and put on cork lifejackets. By the time the whaleboat reached the spot, both the other boats had spilled their crews into the stormy sea. Then McDonald remembered "a big wave came on us and took the stern clean out of the boat and split her from end to end".[19] Mills swam to the ship's lifeboat which, although swamped, had righted itself. McDonald, who could not swim and had no lifebelt, managed to clamber onto a section of the wrecked whaleboat.

Back at the wharf the old lifeboat *Alexandra* was pulled from storage and launched. Lifebelts were tossed into the bottom of the boat; but in the rush to put out to sea they were not put on. The lanyards were not tied to the oars either which cost them dearly because straight after McDonald had been picked up the *Alexandra* capsized, tipping men and oars into the sea. Twice more, as half-drowned men struggled aboard, the lifeboat overturned, throwing them back into the water. When they had picked up everyone they could see, they headed slowly and carefully back to the wharf, Mills giving the crew advice on how to handle the difficult boat. He had stopped using it as it capsized too easily; one of its crew had been drowned the last time it was out. As they reached calm waters, Collis passed out. Cheering crowds greeted survivors and their rescuers at the steps.

The excitement did not last. There were people missing and no one was sure who or how many. While the survivors were wrapped in blankets and helped or carried to the Royal Hotel – Collis and McDonald dangerously exhausted – and Mills was carried back to his house, a fresh crew of volunteers including two of the rocket brigade was found for the *Alexandra*. One of the landing service surf boats had set off to offer assistance before the Timaru lifeboat had been launched. Three sailors had swum to her but the boat was unwieldy in such seas and in danger of foundering, and had been forced to anchor.

It was now dusk and those watching could no longer see what was happening. Out in the bay, some of the men had transferred from the surf boat to the port's lifeboat when the *Alexandra* capsized yet again. Five men were swept out of her but only four got back in. George Falgar, who had been clinging for a long time to one of the buoys, disappeared and was drowned. The boat got back to shore without further mishap, but there were still

In memoriam

This monument was erected in memory of those who lost their lives in the wreck of the *Ben Venue* and the *City of Perth*. It stands on the corner of Sophia and Perth Streets in Timaru, looking south.

ATL F-5336-1/2

The rocket brigade

In 1867, the Provincial Government purchased two rocket "guns" for £280 for use in Timaru. The guns were used to fire a line to ships in distress. The voluntary body that used these guns was led by the local harbour master and became known as the Timaru Volunteer Rocket Brigade.

South Canterbury Museum 848

three men in the surf boat. By now they were in a terrible condition – they had to stand in a boat that was no more than an open iron shell for carrying cargo and was now half-full of water. One more call for volunteers went out and seven offered to go. With bright lights from the rocket brigade making a path across the dark water, they managed to rescue the remaining men and get back to the wharf, this time without accident. When they reached the Royal Hotel, they found it set up as a hospital, the survivors laid out in beds with hot water bottles and heated bricks wrapped in flannel while people rubbed their numb arms and legs, trying to get feeling back into them.

On Monday morning, the town faced the full extent of the previous day's disaster. Forty-three men had been brought safely back to shore by the *Alexandra*, but eight men were dead, including their harbour master; and First Officer John Blacklock of the *City of Perth* would die before the end of the week from his injuries. The harbour master's nine-year-old son had watched the rescue without fully understanding the seriousness of the situation. Mills was heard to speak briefly before he was carried from the wharf with Dr Patrick McIntyre. His last words, according to his son, were "Are they all safe?" When they reached the family house the doctor found Mills was dead. Artificial respiration had no effect. The cause of death was given as "shock to his nervous system caused by immersion in the sea while in discharge of his duty".

> **The *Timaru Herald* published a furious editorial criticising the board for "squabbling for months over the meanest trifles and totally ignoring important business while one big ship is wrecked after another"; and being "obstinately prejudiced against any advice or suggestion from the public, and whose mind is entirely occupied by personal crochets, jealousies and grudges".[20] It finished by accusing the board of putting such pressures on their harbour master he felt forced to take the actions he did, actions which had cost him his life.**

The board held a number of meetings over the next few days. While the town was in mourning, flags flying at half-mast, the board was criticising Mills' actions. All shops and businesses closed on the day of his funeral when nearly 700 people took part in the funeral procession. Captain Sutter chose that same day to tell the board he had never seen "a more reckless sacrifice of human life". He compared the disregard of life in going out to the *City of Perth* with the charge of the Light Brigade at Balaclava.[21] The newspaper was filled with angry letters saying the board had shown itself unfit for business and condemning it for "taunting the life out of Captain Mills" and trying to ruin the reputation of their harbour master. After a fiery public meeting on Friday 19 May, three members of the board were burned in effigy at the end of the breakwater.

The *City of Perth* was refloated, sold and renamed *Turakina*, but the *Ben Venue* was a total loss. For many years its remains were a common sight on the beach at Caroline Bay. By 1978, the sand was beginning to cover the broken ship and more than 100 years on there is no visible evidence of what took place on that "Black Sunday".

The ARIADNE Agreement

The story of the loss of the yacht *Ariadne* is a mixture of mystery, farce and melodrama, with the whiff of a great con hanging over it all. The action spread over 12 months between the Australian state of New South Wales and the South Island of New Zealand. At its heart was a stranding so tidy the crew stepped from the *Ariadne* to their lifeboat to the shore almost without getting their feet wet.

The Ariadne

Type: schooner-yacht
Built: Gosport, England, 1874
Tonnage: 230 tons
Owner: Thomas Caradoc Kerry
Master: Captain George Mumford
Crew: 12
Destined voyage: Sydney–Port Chalmers
Date of departure: 25 February 1901
Date of wreck: 24 March 1901
Location of wreck: 2.5km south of Waitaki River mouth
Lives lost: none

The *Ariadne* was a large, 230-ton yacht rigged as a fore-and-aft schooner, built in England in 1874 of oak, teak and white elm and copper-fastened throughout. At the time it was wrecked, a local paper described the interior fittings as "handsome without being gorgeous" and said, "She has roomy state rooms, dining room, and drawing room."[1] It was a racing yacht, sleek and fast – a "19th century equivalent of a private jet".[2] When it was first built it was said to be the largest schooner-yacht flying the English flag. It had sailed under the Royal Thames Yacht Club's colours and won the German Emperor's Cup at Cowes. But schooner-rigged yachts went out of fashion and in the late 1890s it was sold by Lady Ingram to an Englishman, Thomas Caradoc Kerry, for 2000 guineas – £2100 – a price the new owner described as "more a gift than a purchase".[3]

On 25 February 1901, the *Ariadne* set sail from Sydney for New Zealand. Its destination was the Otago harbour, Port Chalmers, a four-week voyage. There it was to be reprovisioned. Thomas Kerry engaged a new crew and captain, but was unable to accompany them because of business in Sydney. Four weeks later, shortly after 8pm on Sunday 24 March, the man at the helm saw breakers. Minutes later as the lookout ran back from the bow shouting "We're on the beach," the yacht ran aground and then swung round smoothly until broadside on to the shore. The crew collected their belongings, got into the lifeboat and stepped straight out of it into water just over their knees. They only had to wade a few steps. No one was hurt; no one died.

At the nautical inquiry that followed, the 12-man crew were reported to be unfamiliar with the coast, the master's charts were considered inadequate, the dangerous currents of that area of the east coast were emphasised, the crew's competency and discipline questioned along with the quantity and quality of the sails, and the lockers used to store plate, linen and furniture were found

North Otago Museum M23/7

A tidy stranding

"… the poor old *Ariadne* went like spots. There must have been an awful strong current on the coast about there." However, the yacht's master never satisfactorily explained how the vessel ended up in a position that ultimately caused its wrecking.

to be empty. The difference between the actual position of the boat and the position where the master thought it was on the day of the wreck was approximately 48 kilometres,[4] a variance never properly explained. After the hearing, the captain of the *Ariadne*, George Mumford, was judged "negligent of his owner's interest and his manifest duty" and found guilty of "a grave error of judgement when navigating this ship on the 24th of March".[5] His certificate of competency under the Board of Trade was suspended for three months and he was ordered to pay £15 15s towards the total cost of the case – £64.

The yacht lay high on the shingle for a month and despite complicated plans by the Lyttelton agent for Lloyd's to refloat it, that became increasingly unlikely. The vessel was struck heavily by the sea at high tide for several days, stripping away most of the hull's protective copper sheathing on the seaward side. While police guarded it against looters, the Kai Tahu from the Waitaki reserve made the most of this unexpected opportunity and charged visitors a toll to get a close look at the beached ship.

A month after it ploughed into the high shingle bank, two and a half kilometres south of the Waitaki River, it was sold at auction to Port Chalmers shipping agent John Mill for £215. Mill said later that the yacht's value afloat if it was used for commercial work would be £2000, while as a pleasure yacht it "depended upon who wanted her".[6] He never had a chance to find out. A few days later very heavy seas began pounding the *Ariadne* again and within a short time it was smashed to pieces. But Mill was not out of pocket: he salvaged the masts and had access to the lead ballast and pig iron – almost 50 tons of lead at £11 15s a ton and 100 tons of pig iron worth £4 per ton.

The yacht's former owner, Thomas Kerry, had told the newspapers just after the yacht was wrecked that it was valued at £15,000 and that as well as being insured with Lloyd's for £10,000, he held £10,000 insurance on the vessel. At the marine inquiry in April 1901 he informed the court it was worth £20,000; but the Lloyd's surveyor, Stewart Willis, put the value closer to £5000. A substantial part of the lengthy evidence given dealt with the question of whether the ship was "designedly stranded", even though the accusation was not included in the original charge laid by the collector of customs. The court found "there [was] no evidence worthy of the name" to support the allegation of deliberately wrecking the yacht. But Oamaru rumour still suggested this was no accidental loss but a matter of defrauding Lloyd's for the insurance.

Stewart Willis had never been convinced by Captain Mumford's evidence. He found the loss of the only chart Mumford used too convenient – the master claimed it was burnt after a kerosene lamp fell over when the ship struck the shore. What he heard now raised all his old suspicions. The Lloyd's representative in Dunedin, who had earlier employed him to investigate the wreck, now told him to reopen investigations and he began exchanging information with a Detective Fitzgerald.

In late May, Willis received a telegram from the policeman saying that after doing salvage work for John Mill on the wreck, Mumford had left for Dunedin. Fitzgerald was following and suggested Willis should come down to Dunedin too; he would arrange a meeting between the *Ariadne*'s last master and the insurance surveyor. When the detective met Willis off the train, he told him that Mumford had been talking a lot and

**The owner –
Thomas Caradoc Kerry**

Despite a marine inquiry finding that there was no evidence the *Ariadne* was "designedly stranded", public rumour said otherwise.

**The master –
George Mumford**

The Lloyd's representative — Captain Stewart Willis

The insurance assessor always believed the wrecking was an insurance scam, but in the end he could not prove it.

was extremely discontented with Thomas Kerry for not sending him money. He suggested that if Willis "tackled him himself he would get the truth out of Mumford".[7]

The following morning Fitzgerald brought Mumford to Willis at the Grand Hotel and left them together. The surveyor asked him point blank how the *Ariadne* came to be wrecked. Mumford did not reply. Willis tried again. "…He asked whether it would not be better to stick with him (Willis) than to Kerry who had got him to risk his life and those of others and then left him in the lurch. Further pressed by the question, 'Did you or did you not wreck the *Ariadne*?' Mumford said, 'I am sick of Kerry. I will tell you the whole thing tomorrow.'"[8] At this point Willis said the yacht's master was very agitated and so he turned the talk to "general matters". Mumford returned the next day, 29 May, at 11am and for the next hour he told Willis his story.

He said he was introduced to Kerry in Sydney at the beginning of 1901 by a seaman he had known for a couple of years, Andrew Olsen. Olsen had met Kerry on Thursday Island off the northern tip of Cape York Peninsula where the Englishman was waiting for his vessel. Olsen had joined the *Ariadne*'s crew for the voyage down the east coast of Australia. They arrived in Sydney in November 1900, mooring in Neutral Bay, and some weeks later Kerry employed Olsen to work on the yacht's sails. Olsen knew Kerry was looking for a new crew and Mumford came to work on the yacht. Twelve days later, Kerry appointed him master and engaged a crew while the boat was readied for sea. It was then, Mumford told Willis, that Kerry had asked him to wreck the yacht and offered him a substantial sum of money as an inducement. Mumford was hard up and eventually agreed. It was just as Willis had suspected. Mumford explained that New Zealand had been chosen for the wrecking because the insurance policy was due to expire and there was no time to reach a more out of the way place. He assured Willis that "the lifeboat was carefully fitted out, the original intention being to wreck her on the west coast of New Zealand; but this plan had to be abandoned in consequence of the lifeboat being lost during heavy weather on the voyage over".[9] The well-provisioned boat was washed out of its davits in stormy seas shortly after they sighted Cape Farewell.[10]

Willis told Mumford he had to have the story in writing. Mumford refused, and only agreed after Willis promised to pay him. He returned again the next day and wrote out a statement:

> "…I was to receive £12 a month until she was wrecked. I was to be given £200 when the job was done and £200 more when Kerry received the insurance from the underwriters. I agreed to this arrangement, and eventually wrecked the yacht on the Waitaki beach…. The idea was that after I made a total wreck of the *Ariadne* (and it was agreed that it must be a total loss), I was to go Home to England, and he was to find the means of getting me a yachting certificate if my certificate was suspended. Kerry was then going to get hold of another yacht of much more value, insure her heavily, and I was to take her out and wreck her

in the Magellan Strait, and was to get £1000 down as a security and a much larger sum if I made a total loss of her.... All yards of the *Ariadne* were left in Sydney, and I sent all my clothes and valuables on shore, not wishing to lose them. I have witnesses who overheard a great portion of the arrangement made between myself and Kerry. Young E.J. Freke was present with Kerry when our arrangements were made, but he is a confidential friend of Kerry's, and not likely to divulge anything. – George Mumford. 30/5/01"[11]

The price for putting this damning tale in writing was £400 – the reward Mumford told Willis he had been promised, but not yet paid. For his part, Willis also undertook not to tell the police. He told the court later that his instructions from Lloyd's were "on no account to bring a criminal action, but simply to collect evidence to defend a civil action if one was brought".[12] The insurance surveyor now had the instrument of the fraud, but he wanted the instigator. Over the next few days he pressed Mumford for any kind of letter or document that proved Kerry's part in the deception. The captain said there had been an agreement between him and Kerry but he had lost it. He said he had written several letters to Kerry asking for money but Kerry never replied personally, only through his friend Eric Freke.

As Willis maintained his pressure for something more incriminating, Mumford offered to write another letter demanding his money and let Willis see it before he sent it to Sydney. The letter was, in Willis's words, "an extraordinary document":[13]

"Again I write to ask you to forward me some more money and if I do not receive it by return mail I must, in justice to myself, consider our arrangements cancelled re the wreck of the yacht *Ariadne* for you, and I shall consider myself perfectly justified in taking measures to recompense myself in a way that will be at the least very disagreeable to you, and will cost you considerably more than the few hundred pounds you agreed to pay me for risking my life and the lives of others by wrecking the yacht. I may also mention that you do not hold all the 'trump cards'. I admit I have no written agreement from you agreeing to pay me to wreck the yacht. I know you were sharp enough not to do that, but I also have a certain amount of experience in such matters, and generally prepare myself for such little emergencies as these. I am sure you will not blame me, considering two friends of mine were present unknown to you in Sydney at one of our private conversations, and are in possession of just enough to guard against any funny work on your part. But, besides these two, I have a friend in New Zealand who is also acquainted with the whole business, although at the time I did not know he was living, so you see, my dear Mr Kerry, it is not wise to what is vulgarly termed 'act the goat', as you are doing."[14]

The "friend" – Eric John Hussey Freke

The young seaman's close friendship with the *Ariadne*'s owner, an unusual mixing of social classes at that time, placed him in the dock with Kerry and Mumford.

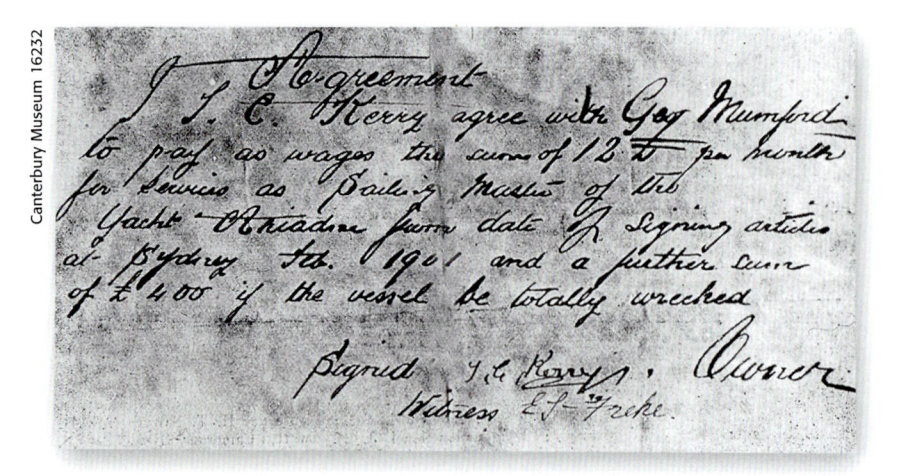

The Agreement

Mumford's copy of the agreement between him and Kerry — it fooled some of the best handwriting experts.

Willis took the threatening letter to the Lloyd's office to have a copy made and certified; and a few days later Mumford went north to Christchurch where he called himself Captain G. Stevens, to prevent Kerry tracing him, he said. Willis had not given up asking for documents that would implicate Kerry in the wreck, and on 7 June Mumford arrived with the agreement he said he had lost. It read:

"I, T.C. Kerry, agree with George Mumford to pay as wages the sum 12£ per month for services as Sailing Master of the Yacht Ariadne from date of signing articles at Sydney Feb. 1901, and a further sum of £400 if the vessel be totally wrecked."[15]

It was signed by both men and witnessed by Freke. The paper had turned up in the lining of an old coat Mumford told him. When Willis pointed out that the letter to Kerry had said there was no written agreement, the captain said he was referring to Kerry's refusal to give him another agreement after Mumford "foolishly" told him he had lost the original. Kerry, he said, observed that without the document "he had no hold on him".[16] Willis immediately had the signatures checked against those on the depositions for the nautical inquiry. They were authenticated. Lloyd's paid Mumford board and "pocket money" during the two months he stayed in Christchurch, and the promised £400 in three instalments, the last on 19 July. Mumford then moved to Lyttelton and went to work on the wharves.

On 8 October, George Mumford was arrested. In Sydney, late that same day, Thomas Caradoc Kerry and Eric John Hussey Freke were also arrested. All three were charged with conspiracy "in casting away the yacht *Ariadne*".[17]

Three days later, Mumford returned to the Christchurch Magistrate's Court on three additional charges — "casting away the ship in concert with Freke; having at Sydney, with Kerry… and Freke, formed the common intention to cast away the ship; and having at Sydney, with the other two, conspired to defraud the underwriters".[18] Much against his will, Willis had been forced to reveal what he knew to the police.

When the men appeared before a packed Magistrate's Court in Christchurch at the end of October, the magistrate, Dr McArthur, agreed with one of the defence counsel who described the evidence as "polluted" but said despite its "unwholesome character" he would not be doing his duty if he did not refer the case to a higher court. The Grand Jury and Mr Justice Denniston at the Supreme Court agreed there was a case to be heard:

"…against Mumford there was his full admission, which incriminated both Kerry and Freke, but which was not admissible as evidence of the complicity of Kerry and Freke…. [There was] the suspicious circumstances connected with the wreck, the fact that she was wrecked in fair weather at a place where she had no business to be, and that at the time of the wreck she was practically denuded of everything. As against Kerry, there was also the same suspicious circumstances…. As against Freke, they had his signature to the agreement. They had the fact that he was on board the ship when she was wrecked and when all the suspicious circumstances occurred, and they had also the fact that he had been in close intimacy with Kerry from the time of the wreck until the present."[19]

The case of deliberately wrecking a ship was a first for New Zealand, "full of interest for the legal mind",[20] and a formidable array of legal talent lined up for the prosecution and defence. The prosecution lawyers for the Crown were Walter Stringer (later knighted) and Michael Myers (a future Chief Justice). For the defence, Kerry was represented by Charles Skerrett (also later a Chief Justice) and Charles Hanlon (a future King's Counsel and one of New Zealand's best-known criminal defence lawyers), whom he had first retained for the nautical inquiry; Mumford was defended by George Harper (knighted later); and Harry Harvey and J. A. Cassidy appeared for Freke. The trial judge was Mr Justice Denniston, afterwards Sir John Denniston.

George Mumford, the man whose statement to Willis and articles of agreement with Kerry had precipitated the court case, was a 38-year-old master mariner, and the only certified officer on board the *Ariadne* for her last voyage. Three weeks before the case was due to begin in the Supreme Court, he complicated matters further when he was discovered trying to bribe a Crown witness, Annie Downing, from giving evidence against him and Kerry. Downing, a barmaid, maintained she overheard Kerry and Mumford arranging to wreck the *Ariadne* while she was serving them in a small private bar in the Port Jackson Hotel in Sydney's George Street. She said she overheard Kerry say, "It's this way, Mumford. I will give you £400 to take the yacht out and lose her." And Mumford had replied, "It's a bargain. I'll do it."[21]

Thomas Kerry was 40, an adventurer born in Cheshire, England. He told reporters:

> "I have travelled a good deal, and though I don't say it boastfully, few people in Christchurch have been further or have seen as much of the world as I can claim to have seen. I am an explorer – that is really my calling, or hobby, as you please to term it. I have seen a good deal of exploring in the South Sea Islands, in the Australian interior, and in New Guinea. I went with the Royal Geographical Society's relief exploring party to New Guinea, and in 1884 was with the Melbourne Age expedition, when our ship was captured by the natives. Have I been in New Zealand before? Oh yes. I have been everywhere on earth very nearly."[22]

For the defence – Charles Hanlon

Hanlon's concentrated study of the damning agreement proved the saving of his client Thomas Kerry. He also had good knowledge of the sea and sailing. He had once considered a naval career and studied astronomy and navigation and held a river-limit captain's certificate.

Later as a ship owner he was involved in trading – everything from black pearls to blackbirding (slave trading). In the hotels and bars around the Sydney waterfront where he was known as "the millionaire" he was usually seen in a straw hat and was described by Annie Downing as "looking rather shabby, but [he] never did look well dressed".[23] He had seen the inside of courts before: in a dispute with a diamond merchant in London, in a case pending in Australia, and in a suit against the *Auckland Star* for libel after they insinuated that he had wrecked the *Harold* and committed theft. He had recently been detained by the French authorities in Noumea; and had been charged with misrepresentation when a company, formed in response to his claim of finding gold in New Guinea, collapsed after he was accused of buying the gold nugget from a jeweller. He was also being sued for breach of promise by two former business partners to recover the money they had invested in what was meant to have been an island trading venture with the *Ariadne*. Kerry had unilaterally decided instead to invest their money in property in Australia. He was counter-suing them for libel.

Eric Freke was much younger than the other two, an 18-year-old midshipman who had been at sea four years, and energetically defended by Kerry as "a gentleman [who] had harmed no one in this world… entirely innocent of any crime or criminal intention".[24] He had known Kerry for about two years after meeting him in London where, he said, they were introduced by the Duke of Manchester. He had told the nautical inquiry "he did not know where the yacht was going when he asked for the job [and] considered it was a mere act of friendship"[25] that Kerry gave him the job. He did not expect or intend to ask for any wages. The Sydney policeman who arrested them found them lodging at the same house and sharing a room.

The final act in what had become known as the *Ariadne* case began at the Christchurch Supreme Court on 20 January 1902 with the three defendants accused of "casting away the sailing yacht *Ariadne*". All pleaded not guilty. Mumford's written statement to Stewart Willis was excluded from evidence because the £400 payment made the truth of it legally suspect. But there were other statements – Mumford's first verbal statement to Willis and the conversations he had directly with witnesses, or which were overheard.

> **Annie Downing not only claimed to have heard Kerry and Mumford talking about wrecking the yacht, she had also had several conversations with Mumford about it afterwards. The last, where he said that if she came over to their side she "would be paid so much down and so much after the case was over",[26] was witnessed by two policemen hidden behind a curtain in the corner of the room, and he was arrested.**

Mumford also had a problem with his friend Andrew Olsen – Mumford told Downing they had offered him £20 not to testify "but he was too frightened".[27] According to Olsen, Kerry had asked him to join the *Ariadne* as first mate but he was not prepared to pay

Olsen's rate – £8 a month. Once Mumford was captain, he asked Olsen repeatedly to join him as mate and mentioned the wrecking, saying "the job had to be done in a month, for the insurance had nearly run out and then they would get nothing".[28] He offered him £20 out of his share. Olsen refused. Then when Kerry returned to Sydney after the inquiry into the wreck, he sought out Olsen and told him the accusations were "all nonsense" and he had lost £10,000. Olsen said Kerry came to see him almost every day, "treating" him and getting him jobs until Olsen left Sydney for England in July. The court was also read a letter Mumford had sent Olsen at the end of May:

> "…the poor old *Ariadne* went like spots. There must be an awful strong current on the coast about there. I wish you had come with me instead of that soft second chump I had to take over. You know something about the coast, and we might have got along without getting wrecked. I have got some good news for you, old man, which you will be pleased to hear; and there is money in it for you, but it is too private to write about. You can perhaps guess what it is about, so do not go gassing about until I see you."[29]

The only reason Olsen could think of for receiving money from Mumford was because the *Ariadne*'s captain did not want him to talk about the yacht.

One of the men who did sail with the yacht, able seaman Hermann Wynd, claimed he overheard a conversation between the owner and master on the deck the day before they sailed. He heard Kerry say, "Do you remember our agreement? £400 for you if you make this right. For God's sake don't make a mess of it. Pile her up somewhere. Do anything to get rid of her. I have paid that much insurance."[30] He described how the lifeboat had been worked on every day on the trip over, until it was lost overboard; and how the evening before they departed he had seen a boat go ashore filled with boxes and trunks. He admitted that later on the voyage he quarrelled with Mumford who tried to hit him.

The man who briefly stored the goods taken from the ship, about two tonnes in all, said some of the parcels were so heavy two men were needed to lift them, and among them he saw what he thought were a couple of binnacle lamps, a sextant and chronometer case, and some guns.

The crew
Members of the *Ariadne*'s crew back on the yacht before it broke up. Below, a more formal portrait, lined up against a painted sea.

SHIPWRECK

The third day of the hearing opened sensationally. The Crown Prosecutor said he wished to make a statement. The agreement at the centre of the case, he said, was a forgery and so the case against Freke "fell to the ground". It also removed the only documentary piece of evidence linking Kerry to the wrecking. Defense lawyer Hanlon had employed some clever sleuthing after seeing a copy of the agreement, minus the clause about wrecking, found among Kerry's papers. He arranged to have Mumford's copy photographed and then had substantial enlargements made. When they were projected onto a screen they showed the main text had been traced over and there were "tell-tale signs of uneven inking on all words save the final twelve".[31] The charge against Freke was withdrawn and he was discharged immediately.

The next day a waiter from Mumford's Christchurch hotel told the court he had seen Mumford working on a document headed "Agreement" and had been told "it was important work and [Mumford] had to magnify every word".[32] Mumford and his agreement were now totally discredited. He was not just a confessed wrecker who attempted to bribe witnesses, but in Hanlon's words also "a liar, a perjurer, and a forger".[33]

On the fifth day, the case came to a close and the lawyers summed up for the jury. Mumford's counsel, struggling to put a good light on his client's case, said that his confession must have been a fraud from beginning to end and that there was no evidence that he wilfully wrecked the yacht. "If they came to the conclusion there was no evidence to connect Kerry, then there was nothing to show that Mumford had wilfully wrecked the yacht."[34] Hanlon, closing Kerry's defence, scoffed at the idea that conspirators would have incriminating conversations where they could be easily overheard and in front of witnesses. If one part of the evidence was paid for, he said, it was likely other parts were also; and if one part was false then it was likely other parts were just as false. Stringer, for the Crown, described the evidence as a maze of trickery and fraud through which it was "his duty simply to assist the jury".

After a brief two hours, the jury returned their verdict. Mumford was found guilty and sentenced to four years' hard labour. Kerry, however, was acquitted on all charges. He said later the case against him had been "the dirtiest, meanest and most contemptible thing I ever heard of" and claimed after the verdict "hundreds of people of all classes – people whom I have never seen before to my knowledge – shook me warmly by the hand".[35] But many of those who had followed the case's tortuous twists and turns were surprised he had got away scot-free while Mumford received such a harsh sentence.

After his acquittal, Kerry refused to divulge his future plans saying they were "very indefinite", but when Lloyd's still refused to pay out he returned to England with Freke and settled the matter there. Nevertheless the question of guilt continued to hang over him. Some years later he came back to New Zealand and in 1927 bought the Wenderholm estate north of Auckland. He was rumoured to keep a loaded gun and became increasingly reclusive. George Mumford was sent to Hanmer Springs prison where he cleared scrub and planted trees. On 8 October 1904, he was released early for good behaviour. Later he was based in Papua New Guinea and died several years before Kerry.

"The principals of the case"

The three defendants on a break in the proceedings: Eric Freke, Thomas Kerry (holding his hat in front of his face), and Captain Mumford — all on the steps of the courthouse. Mumford was the only one to spend time in prison.

ADRiFT –
The Lost Survivors of the
ELiNGAMiTE

The Elingamite set out from Sydney in fair conditions, but during Friday afternoon, a fine sea haze closed in. All day Saturday the steamer sailed in a thick mist. On Sunday morning, many passengers were up on deck soon after breakfast hoping for their first glimpse of land. For vessels on the Sydney–Auckland run this was usually the western island in the Three Kings group, which lies some 50 kilometres west-north-west of Cape Maria Van Dieman. Ships took their bearings from the Three Kings for the final leg of their journey down the coast to Auckland. But this Sunday morning, with the ship wrapped in dense fog, visibility was reduced to a bare two ships' lengths.

At 9am, the engines were cut to half speed and a lookout posted. The fog horn began blowing at two-minute intervals, a finger of sound stretching into the blanket of fog probing for an indication of land. At 10am, with weather conditions "thick as a ditch" according to Len Burkitt, the chief officer, and visibility no more than a few metres,

SS Elingamite

Type:	steel screw passenger steamer
Built:	Newcastle, England, 1887
Length:	94.48 metres (310 feet)
Beam:	12.33 metres (40 feet 8 inches)
Depth:	5.9 metres (19 feet 7 inches)
Tonnage:	2585 tons gross
Owner:	Huddart Parker Ltd, Melbourne
Master:	Captain E. B. Attwood
Crew:	58
Passengers:	136
Cargo:	large general cargo, 850 tons coal, timber, 52 boxes silver and gold coins to value of £17,320, 22 bags of mail.
Destined voyage:	Sydney–Auckland
Date of departure:	5 November 1902
Date of wreck:	9 November 1902
Location of wreck:	West Island, Three Kings Islands
Lives lost:	45

The *Elingamite*

Early in September 1902, a young Sydney woman had a dream. She saw a man being lowered from a ship onto some rocks. The scene changed: now she was surrounded by rocks. As the dream unravelled, she saw sailing ships and then a small cottage on a hill. Some three weeks later, she embarked on her first sea voyage to visit her brother in New Zealand. Less than an hour after weighing anchor, she watched with other passengers on the steamer *Elingamite* as a stowaway was put off at Garden Island, just inside the heads to Sydney Harbour. As the man was lowered onto boulders along the shore, she recognised the scene and her half-forgotten dream flashed back. The first part of it had just been played out. The young woman, Miss Alice May Maybee, was among 136 passengers on board the *Elingamite* when it left Sydney late on Wednesday afternoon, 5 November 1902, at the start of a regular five-day run to Auckland.

Auckland City Libraries A14309

Captain Ernest Bacot Attwood ordered the ship's speed reduced to dead slow. Creeping forward at four and a half knots, it seemed to some of those on deck that the ship had almost stopped moving.

Attwood knew he must be close to the Three Kings. According to the charts and by his estimates, the *Elingamite* had passed them and was six or seven miles (10-11 kilometres) south of the island group. While the men on lookout and the captain and third mate on the bridge strained to see into the thick air around them, Sunday morning ship life continued. Passengers and crew were scattered throughout the steamer. Most of the former – businessmen, holiday makers and immigrants – were below, a few still in their cabins and not yet dressed. However, a good number of passengers were up on deck, chatting, reading, and still hoping for a glimpse of land.

Shortly after 10.30am they got their wish, in a sudden jumble of images. At the rail, Steven Neill, a tram motorman from Newcastle, saw "one of the most beautiful sights my eyes had ever witnessed…. A thick heavy bank of fog had come down the side of a hill. It did not touch the water and was clear enough for 20 yards or 30 yards high. It very much resembled a snow clad mountain. The scene charmed me and for some seconds I stood looking at it. Then the thought struck me that we were making right for it."[1] Hal Henkinson, another motorman, was lying on a rug on a hatchway reading when his wife came running down from the poop deck calling to come and see how close they were to the rocks. "I looked up, and it was just as if a curtain had gone up on some transformation scene. The mist had lifted before us just enough to show an immense rock towering up over our heads."[2]

As the lookout shouted "Breakers ahead" and the bells began ringing for the engines to reverse "full speed astern", passenger Alice Maybee recalled that "the steamer continued to move slowly ahead and a moment later she grated slightly on the reef. This was followed by a great crash, and then all knew that the vessel was doomed. For a moment everyone seemed stricken dumb and unable to do anything…."[3] Down below, able seaman Theodore Danielson heard the lookout cry, "All hands on deck."[4] The *Elingamite* had struck West King Island, tearing a hole in her port side before swinging broadside onto the rocks.

It was immediately obvious the ship could not be saved. Descriptions of what followed vary. Some passengers said that everyone remained calm and orderly with the exception of a group of "foreigners" whom they accused of rushing the lifeboats. Dr Goldie, the older brother of the

ADRiFT –
The Lost Survivors of
THE ELiNGAMiTE

Sea mist over Three Kings

"… a ledge of rock as hard and sharp as rocks are made… the sea roaring on three sides… and the sea birds screaming and screeching all night long…"

Kelly Tarlton's Shipwreck Museum

Life saving voyage

First Officer L.J. Burkitt guided a lifeboat with 52 survivors over 150 kilometres without a compass and in thick fog and night to find safe landfall and bring news of the wreck.

painter Charles Goldie, described "terrified people rushing about, tumbling over one another in an eager search for life-belts. Many did not seem to know where to look for them; others found them already taken from under their pillows, or out of order, and tried in turn to snatch them from others. In the saloon I saw a lady hugging her children, wildly excited and refusing assistance."[5]

The captain believed that he had struck the biggest island, Great King. Its eastern side offered safe landing places. One of the passengers who knew local waters, Captain William Reid, volunteered to take a boat, find a place to land and then return to the ship. His lifeboat carrying 20 people was first away. Within minutes the *Elingamite* was swallowed up in the fog. Among those on the boat was Agnes Robb with her six-year-old son Connal, crippled with spinal TB. Agnes wrote later:

"Once clear of the ship the men pulled round the rocks in search of a landing place, but none could be found. There was no compass to guide us and there were no provisions but a keg of water and a box with the ship's papers. Now and again the fog lifted and we would see another boat and then lose sight of it again as the fog closed round us."[6]

Back on the *Elingamite*, five more lifeboats were launched. The ship was sinking faster than expected. People began jumping overboard, hoping to be picked up by boats already in the water or still being lowered. James McGeorge saw a young couple on deck. "They asked me pitifully what was to be done. I answered that all the boats had gone and they must look after themselves. Just then the ship gave a canting roll and they were shot over the side. I watched, but they never came to the surface. They went down in each other's arms."[7]

Hal Henkinson had managed to place his two-year-old son in a lifeboat but it was launched before his wife and daughter could get in. Now, holding his little girl and surrounded by cries for help, he and his wife struggled through water jammed with wreckage. Once, he and the child were forced under as someone scrambled onto his shoulders to get to the surface. Later a hand grabbed his ankle and clung desperately for a short time. They were finally picked up by one of the last lifeboats to leave the scene. The captain and the first and second mates were the last to leave the ship, washed from their hold on the flying bridge and funnel as the *Elingamite* slid beneath the waves. Less than half an hour had elapsed since they hit the reef. The five lifeboats and two rafts, most of them overladen with survivors, rapidly lost contact with each other.

Attwood had instructed the first and third officers, Burkitt and Watson, to sail their lifeboats for North Cape to raise the alarm. Dr Beattie, Cora Anderson and Hal Henkinson and his wife and daughter were among the 36 passengers and 15 crew in

First Officer Burkitt's lifeboat. They also carried the body of an elderly woman, Mrs Sully, who had died as she was pulled from the water. There was little in the way of provisions on board: just a full beaker of water, and a few oranges and loquats and a case of schnapps they fished out of the sea. With no compass and only a sketchy sense of their position, Burkitt steered the lifeboat clear of the wreckage and headed into the mist. Late in the afternoon, they glimpsed another lifeboat, sails set, some three miles off. Then the sea mist closed again. As night came on, a light rain began to fall.

Attwood was picked up by a lifeboat already in difficulty. It had been holed by wreckage and although the hole was hastily stuffed with men's shirts, water continued to fill the boat. Whisky and schnapps cases pulled from the sea, a bucket and even hats and caps became bailers. Fred Chambers, the purser, in charge of a dinghy with 12 survivors, found his boat also needed constant bailing. "We pulled away a bit and the fog came on thicker and swallowed us up and we lost sight of everything," Chambers said. "We had no compass, nor was there anything to show us in what direction to steer. We pulled about for a while, shouting and coo-eeing, and at last we saw a sail, which proved to be the third mate's boat."[8] Watson told Chambers he was making for land. Then he disappeared again into the fog. Chambers next met up with the two rafts. They attempted to stay together, but the wind and currents were too strong and the rafts, with only a couple of oars and partially submerged, were awkward to manage. The wind was rising and the seas becoming rougher when the large lifeboat with Attwood loomed out of the fog close to Chambers' dinghy. They sailed on, the captain blowing a whistle so they would not lose contact with each other again. At one island, he sent one of the crew ashore to scout a landing spot and was then forced to leave the unfortunate man clinging to rocks with a promise to return later.

Attwood was heading for another possible landing place when the people on Captain Reid's lifeboat caught sight of them and set sail to join them. "[T]he men were rowing by this time, such squalls came upon us when we heard Captain Attwood's whistle and we took it to mean that he had found a landing," Agnes Robb wrote.

> "There were some people scrambling on the ledge of rock as we approached. Imagine a narrow inlet, the sea having broken through the cliffs on one side, a ledge of rock as hard and sharp as rocks are made, some twenty feet above sea level, the sea roaring on three sides, the spray dashing up on the ledge and the sea birds screaming and screeching all night long, with fog and rain in addition? Ah me! I never wish to hear these sounds again – dreary, cruel, desolate, eerie."[9]

The 67 survivors from the three boats struggled ashore, cold, wet, hungry and exhausted. It was late afternoon. They had been searching for a place

Fatal errors
Captain Attwood not only had inaccurate charts to navigate by, he also made a mistake in reading sea currents, taking his ship even further from a safe course.

Kelly Tarlton's Shipwreck Museum

The survivors

Survivors from the *Elingamite* finish their journey to Auckland on the *Zealandia*. Top left, those who reached Hohoura with Burkitt; top right, the occupants of Captain Attwood's boat. Bottom left, the men from the No.1 raft who landed at Great King; bottom right, those picked up by Chambers in the small dinghy.

to land for six hours. Using sails from the lifeboats, the men rigged up a rough cover. They had no food, just a case of brandy and a keg of water which were doled out at intervals among the women and children. Agnes Robb had saved a few raisins from dinner on Saturday which she gave to Connal. It was a miserable night.

Only one other group found land that day. Eleven men on the smaller raft had drifted out into open sea when the fog lifted for a few minutes and they saw land about eight kilometres behind them. They changed course, rowing four to an oar into the wind against a strong current and with waves breaking over them. They knew that if they did not find land before dark they probably never would. Ninety minutes later, they were outside the reef to the Great King. "Here we had a terrific struggle, pulling for a little haven," James McGeorge said. "It was against wind and tide…. It was dead low water and there were no breakers or else we could not have got ashore. We walked on shore and gave three heartfelt cheers. Then we wrote out a message on the raft: 'Eleven passengers cast away on the Greater King.' The raft went in a straight course for the mainland…. We slept on the rocks for the night. Dr Goldie put his arms round my neck and hugged me like a child to keep warmth in me."

At daybreak on Monday, Attwood and Reid set out to row back to the wreck area to check for survivors and to salvage food if possible. The weather had worsened. It defeated Attwood and his men, despite several hours "warring with tides and currents". Reid was more successful. First he picked up the crewman left behind in the search for a suitable landing place. "It was an awful job to get him off," Reid recalled. "The sea was breaking in and washing clean over him." At the wreck site, the fog was still thick. There was plenty of wreckage but little food. They retrieved two cases of gin and a few onions and oranges.

The raft party
Steven Neill (above), one of only eight survivors from the 16 who set out on the large raft (below), tried to ease his terrible thirst by sucking on a small coin.

> "We saw a number of bodies… and this gruesome sight much upset my men who had been pulling heroically for eleven hours… in a heavy gale of wind. The men were beginning to give way. Their hands were completely worn, they were gone at the wrists…."[10]

The Three Kings' notoriously difficult conditions now stopped Reid and his men from returning to those waiting for them. After repeated attempts to reach the shore, he caught sight of another island through the fog and recognised its outline as the Great King. They turned for there instead and found the survivors from the small raft.

SHIPWRECK

The other lifeboats at sea that morning were Watson's and Burkitt's heavily laden craft. Some time during the night, Burkitt had sighted the Southern Cross through the fog and clouds and set a course by it. The following morning the fog lifted and at 8 o'clock they saw land for the first time. Shortly after noon, they beached the boat near the small Maori settlement of Te Kowhai. It was 25 hours since being wrecked and they had sailed over 150 kilometres. They rested at Te Kowhai and went across to Hohoura the next day. When the news reached Auckland, the telegraph office and the local agents for the shipping company were besieged. As the list of survivors from Burkitt's boat was read out, men wept and women fainted. Over the next 12 hours, four ships were dispatched to search for those still missing. When John Robb learned Agnes and Connal were not among the 52 survivors, he got a passage on the *Clansman*, the first and fastest ship to leave Auckland in the search.

At the Three Kings, conditions had not improved for his wife and son. "The fog continued all Monday with roaring seas," Agnes said. "Many attempts were made to scale the cliffs in hope of finding birds' eggs, but in vain. A few sticks were found and one or two dry matches… and a fire kindled. In the bailer were boiled such shellfish as could be picked from the rocks and all the crabs that could be found. Connal and I let the crabs pass that day – by Tuesday we were ready for our share. About 5pm we settled down for another night. We thought of the other boats and rafts. Our hope lay with the first mate's boat which was to make for the mainland – Cape Maria Van Dieman – whence word might be sent to Auckland and we reckoned how soon we might look for rescue…. We lost our two boats that night, they broke from their moorings…. There was a good deal of fainting and hysteria on the part of some women that night and much wailing on the part of children for the food that might not be had."[11]

Tuesday brought the first improvement in their conditions. The fog lifted and the sun shone in a blue sky. They saw the Great King opposite and for the first time knew where they were. They cooked some fish caught on lines made from corset laces with hat pins for hooks. But when two sailing ships were sighted, their fires and flags made from petticoats and shirts went unnoticed. The ships sailed on. Across on Great King the men had been able to get off the rocky ledge where they spent their first night. On Monday morning, with a rope saved from the raft, they scaled the cliff behind them. While Dr Goldie and another man searched and failed to find a government food depot for shipwreck survivors, others tried equally

Castaway ingenuity

Those who landed on the islands had to improvise to survive. On Great King men without boots cut makeshift sandals from lifebelts and tied them to their feet with handkerchiefs. Across on another island they caught fish with hooks made from hat pins dangled on corset laces.

unsuccessfully to light a fire with the glass from watches and by rubbing sticks together. They took the few wet matches they had and rolled the phosphorus into small lumps to remake strikable match heads. The first couple of matches disintegrated and the last match had already lost half its head when James McGeorge made the final attempt – "… amidst a shout of joy the remaining portion of the match suddenly blazed into fire, and fell into a heap of dry leaves… we piled on dry tea-tree and dry leaves and soon had a big blazing bonfire."[12]

They were up very early on Tuesday morning, convinced the *Zealandia* would sail by. "We hailed a sailing ship early but got no response," McGeorge remembered.

> "The forecabin steward went and discovered a spring [their first good water] and got two bottles of water for the crowd and as we were having a drink the chief steward saw smoke on the horizon. We did cheer, I can tell you, and yelled out to the other fellows to set fire to the tussocks. They did not seem to see at first, so we set fire to the whole side of the hill, including [our] hut. Then they saw us and blew the syren."[13]

The ship was the *Zealandia* en route to Sydney. It had been hailed by a whaling boat from Hohoura about six on Tuesday morning and changed course for the Three Kings immediately. It took several hours for all the survivors to be picked up from the two islands. The steamer then circled the wreck area before starting back for Auckland. Despite the rapturous welcome the survivors received on their return, there were still many people missing. Watson's boat with 30 passengers and the large raft with 16 people on board had been seen last on Sunday afternoon.

The raft had just one oar, one scull and one rowlock, and when all efforts to fight the currents and tides failed, they had dropped a sea anchor – a bag on a rope – and drifted. It was so overloaded it was swamped and the 16 sat up to their waists in water with the sea breaking over them. There was a water keg on board but it turned out to be empty. It served instead as a seat for the only woman among them, Alice McGuirk, a stewardess from the *Elingamite*. On Monday, they put Henry Wetherilt in charge because of his seafaring experience and he divided the first of two apples picked from the water into 16 segments. This was their only food. The weather was foggy and cool that day and the night cold. Three people died before morning and with reluctance they pushed their bodies overboard, lightening the load a little. On Tuesday, the fine weather which had cheered up those on the islands was to prove fatal for some on the raft. "That day the desire for water was overpowering and some

The Robb family

Above, Connal and Douglas Robb. John Robb knew how lucky his family (below) had been when he saw others: "children whose parents were missing, fathers and mothers whose children were missing, wives whose husbands were missing…"

The... Elingamite Disaster.

Ladies' Cricket Match and Garden Party

GIVEN BY...
Williamson's Musical Comedy Company...

In aid of the Sufferers by the above Disaster.

To be held on the
Wellington College Grounds,
By the courtesy of the Governors and Principals of the Wellington College.

Wednesday, 19th November, 1902, at 2.30 p.m.

of the people on the raft began to drink salt water, despite all that could be said of the terrible consequences that might ensue. It was very hard indeed to resist the temptation with the ocean all round us and us dying with thirst, and several times I had to shut my eyes to hide from my view the tempting sight."[14] Later Henry Wetherilt's son gave a brief but graphic description of what his father and the others had been through: "The thirst caused their tongues to protrude like pieces of leather. When the raft would take a dip, as happened constantly, they were drenched, and it was terrific when the sea was running, the occupants of the raft being ducked under the water. They kept imagining they could see things, even at times having the illusion that they espied green trees.... To add to the horror of the situation... the waters through which the raft drifted was infested with sharks."[15]

On Tuesday night one of the men who had been drinking seawater became delirious and jumped overboard before anyone could stop him. On Wednesday, Wetherilt divided the second apple between the remaining 12 and tried to cheer them. Steven Neill tore up and ate his handkerchief to ease his hunger pangs. "During the afternoon another man went mad and jumped overboard, and at night still another slipped over the side and passed from sight, singing," Theodore Danielson said. "We suffered terribly through the night, and before the morning Ellis the second saloon steward had died from exhaustion. In the morning early Mrs. McGuirk, the fore-cabin stewardess, also passed away, dying quietly from exhaustion. She was very depressed and despondent for some time before death. It is a marvel to me that these two managed to hold on to life so long; they were so thin and emaciated."[16] By Thursday afternoon the remaining eight survivors had almost given up hope of being found alive. Then they saw a ship, far away on the horizon.

HMS *Penguin* had been zigzagging north-east of the Three Kings when she sighted wreckage. Next, the lookout noticed a small white object on the skyline. Through his telescope he could see a raft with people on it and Danielson's hastily made flag – a shirt tied to the oar. Shortly after 4pm, the *Penguin* reached them and a boat was lowered. They were helped into it and immediately given small amounts of water, hot Bovril and brandy. The eight men, nearly dead from exposure, had drifted more than 100 kilometres from the Three Kings. On the *Penguin*, sailors and newsmen alike were shocked by the survivors' physical condition:

> "… the skin burnt and blistered on their faces, their eyes bloodshot and strained with salt brine and long gazing over an empty sea for the succour that was so long in coming. Their poor feet and legs, too tender and raw from exposure to saltwater and sun to bear the weight of their coverings, were visible, and it made one shiver to look at them…."[17]

Although ships continued to search the area and people down the coast kept a lookout for Watson's lifeboat, it was never found. Thirty people simply sailed into the fog and disappeared forever. Altogether 45 lives were lost in the wreck of the *Elingamite* – 17 crew and 28 passengers.

On 28 November 1902, a Nautical Court of Inquiry began a six-week hearing into the disaster. Attwood was found guilty of negligent navigation. The court criticised the inadequate lifeboat equipment and poor condition of the tackle, the irregularity of boat drills for the crew and the way the ship's officers failed to keep lifeboats and rafts together after they were launched. It also expressed concern over the uneven allocation of passengers in the lifeboats. Attwood had to pay £50 towards the cost of the inquiry and had his certificate suspended for a year. It was the end of his career at sea. He found work on shore as a tally clerk for a coal company. However, eight years later, Parliament ordered the inquiry reopened after a routine naval survey discovered that the Three Kings were wrongly charted. The *Elingamite* had not been off the accepted course. Attwood was exonerated completely and awarded compensation by the court.

The large amount of gold and silver coins on board the ship when it was wrecked – £17,000 – ensured that the *Elingamite* was not forgotten. Over the next few years, seven different salvage expeditions attempted to recover the money, but it was not until January 1907 that a diver succeeded in bringing up approximately £2500 worth before he collapsed and died from the bends. Then, between 1965 and 1969, three divers – Kelly Tarlton, Wade Doak and John Gallagher – recovered a lot of silver and 21 gold half-sovereigns. They also raised the ship's bell and other pieces from the wreck, but the Three Kings wreck site remains a difficult and dangerous place to dive, the conditions as potentially deadly as they were for the *Elingamite* over 90 years ago.

ADRIFT –
The Lost Survivors of
THE ELINGAMITE

Raising the ship's bell

Kelly Tarlton, Wade Doak and John Gallagher (below) carried out the first successful modern salvage work on the *Elingamite*. Tarlton bought the wreck and continued to raise bullion until his death in 1985.

Kelly Tarlton's Shipwreck Museum

ATL G-16780-1/2 (Kinnear Collection)

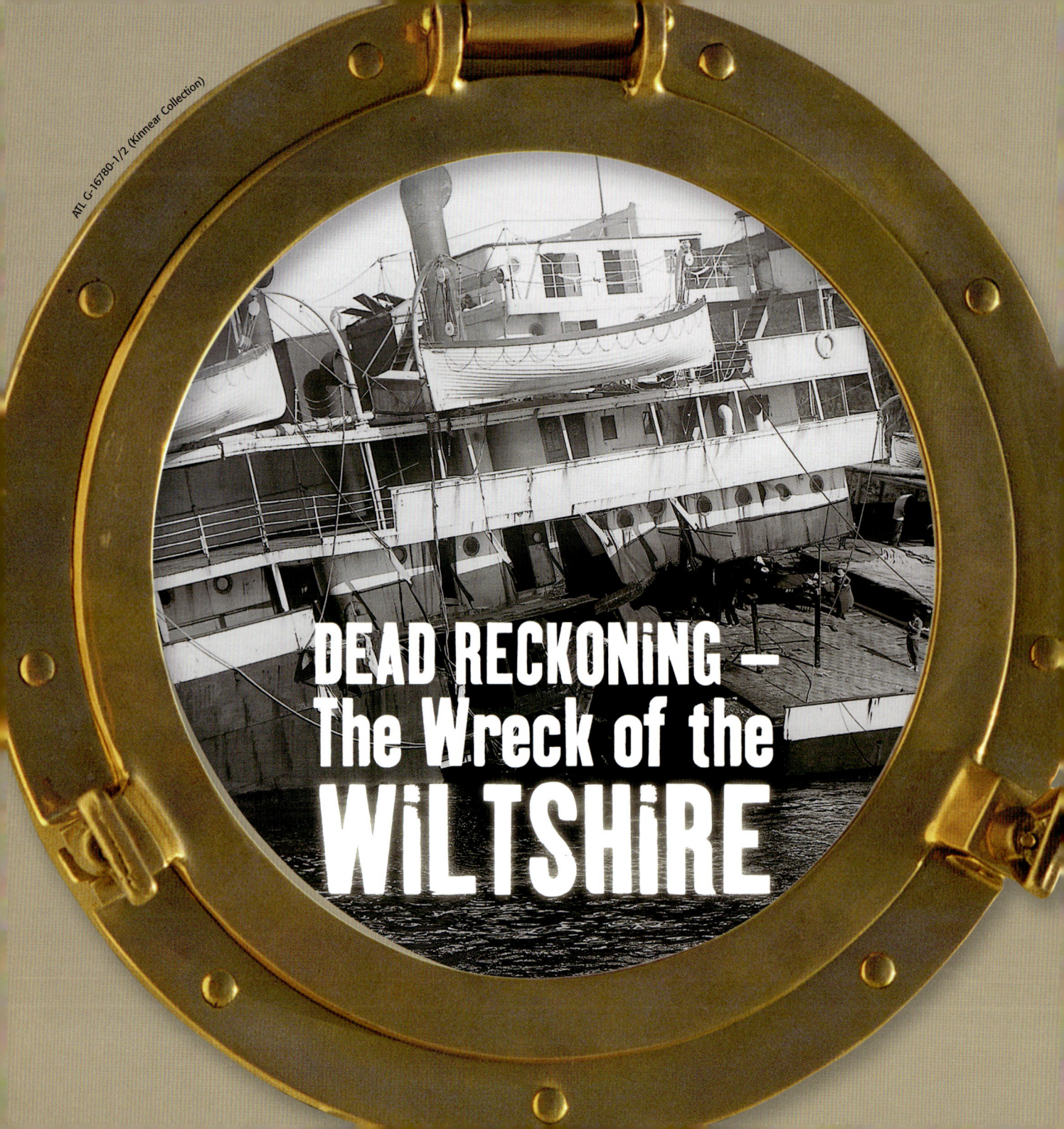

DEAD RECKONING –
The Wreck of the
WiLTSHiRE

When the impact came, the quartermaster was running forward to the bridge with the latest sounding — a mere 70 fathoms. High above him, the lookout in the crow's nest, blinded and deafened by the black night and foul weather, shouted suddenly, "Breakers ahead." But even as he shouted and reached to sound the ship's alarm, J.H. Musgrove[1] felt "a terrible judder, a ringing vibration of the rudder quadrant in the deckhouse beside me and almost simultaneously three shocking bumps that knocked me off my feet. At the same time an oncoming sea slammed into us".[2] As he scrambled to his feet crying "Run for your lives" a great wave engulfed him, picking him up and sweeping him forward, sprawled, along the deck. Overhead, the lookout continued to sound the alarm.

TSS Wiltshire

Type:	twin-screw, five-masted steamer
Built:	John Brown and Company, Clydebank, Glasgow, Scotland, 1912
Port of registry:	London
Length:	160 metres (526 feet 6 inches)
Beam:	19 metres (61 feet 4 inches)
Depth:	11 metres (36 feet 6 inches)
Tonnage:	12,160 tons gross, 7,801 tons net register
Engines:	propulsion twin screw coal burner, quadruple expansion, 2×4CY each 6500 I.H.P.
Owner:	Federal Steam Navigation Company
Master/Commander:	Captain G. Bertram Hayward
Crew:	103, and 1 stowaway
Cargo:	10,000 tonnes general merchandise and 460 postal bags
Destined voyage:	Liverpool–Auckland–Wellington–Lyttelton–Dunedin
Date of departure:	22 April 1922
Date of wreck:	31 May 1922
Location of wreck:	Rosalie Bay, 3 miles north of the southern end of Great Barrier Island
Lives lost:	None

Auckland Museum C3047

The *Wiltshire*

A rare example of a five-masted steamer, the refrigerated passenger cargo vessel was less than seven hours from port when it struck rocks.

Unable to see the other crew on deck in the intense darkness, Third Mate Musgrove fought to regain his feet and made for the bridge. The very thing he had been dreading for the last two hours had happened – the ship had run aground. Faint light from portholes on the lower decks revealed their immediate surroundings. There were rocks close in all around them while immediately in front of the vessel high rocky cliffs rose sheer out of a raging sea. The TSS *Wiltshire* had run straight into the largest island in the Hauraki Gulf, Great Barrier Island. It was a few minutes after 11pm on Wednesday 31 May 1922. On board were a crew of 103 and a stowaway, discovered three days out from Liverpool, too late to put him ashore. For the first time in a long while, the ship carried no passengers.

The vessel now trapped on the rocks had been one of the world's largest passenger/cargo refrigerated ships when it was built in 1911-12, and a rare example of a five-masted steamer. It was specially adapted with a hinged funnel and masts to pass through the great Manchester ship canal. Although it had been hired by the Ministry of Transport to bring home New Zealand servicemen after the First World War, and had traded regularly to Australia, this was its first commercial voyage to New Zealand for the Federal Steam Navigation Company.

The *Wiltshire* took on goods at Avonmouth, Glasgow and Liverpool. In New Zealand, it would load refrigerated cargo for the return trip. The ship left Liverpool on 22 April 1922, sailed through the Panama Canal, then south to Bilboa to replenish its fresh water, and across the Pacific. According to Second Officer Mayo Harris' log, the voyage was uneventful – winds varying from force 3 to force 6, mostly from the east to south-east, with an average sailing speed of just over 12 knots.[3]

They were 20 days out from Bilboa and approaching the Hauraki Gulf when the weather deteriorated: on Monday 29 May, the winds were south south-east force 3.

By late the next day, Wednesday 31 May – one day jumped because of crossing the dateline – they had escalated to force 7. Musgrove remembered they sailed into a cloudy dawn "but at 8 o'clock the sun appeared and we were able to get our sextant sights for longitude. The 'then' position was ascertained, using a calculated latitude which would normally be verified by observing the sun at noon. These later sights were never taken, however, for by mid-morning, with a sharply falling barometer, cloud had begun to cover the sky and we saw no more of the sun."[4] (The ship's master, Captain Bertram Hayward, remembered differently. He believed a midday sighting had been made, according to his evidence to the official inquiry into the wrecking.)

With a rising sea and swell, the ship prepared for filthy weather – closing hatches and battening down round the decks. By 6 o'clock there was a full gale blowing "but with the wind and sea behind us the ship was ambling comfortably along". They were now less than 12 hours from their destination and Captain Hayward telegraphed ahead to alert the port agents that their estimated time of arrival would be 5am the next day. Hayward knew that once preparations for discharging the cargo were made there were costs and penalties if they had to be changed. Every effort was made to arrive on time.

Musgrove came on duty for the first watch at 8pm. Hayward had left one "special" instruction: to call him when the Cuvier Island Light was sighted, or at 10 o'clock if it had not been seen. Cuvier Island lies south-east of Great Barrier, and the island and the beam from its lighthouse are ships' first sightings of Auckland and the entrance to the harbour up Colville Channel. The storm was growing worse. The night was "so thick that the mast light was invisible from the bridge"[5] and the gale was causing an additional problem:

> "For several hours the following wind had been causing a constant downpour of clinker ash on to the bridge from the funnel as the smoke drove rapidly forward, but a more serious factor had now arisen. The wind had changed a point or two to the starboard quarter and the smoke was now tending to obscure our visibility over the port bow where we were expecting to see the Cuvier Light."[6]

At 9.15pm, Musgrove called down the speaking tube to the captain. He told him heavy rain was still falling and the visibility was much worse. Musgrove suggested turning the ship about and keeping out to sea until morning. Hayward said no. However he did order a slight change of course to improve visibility by bringing the smoke broader on the bow. This was a risky decision: they were sailing by dead reckoning and their exact position was uncertain.

Next Musgrove suggested they cut their speed. Hayward rejected the idea. At 9.45pm, Musgrove took a depth sounding although the commander thought it unnecessary. The third mate was not working under ideal conditions – the ship's gear was slow and inaccurate and they were travelling at speed. Nevertheless, he got an ominous reading of 85 fathoms. The seabed shelves steeply off this part of the coast and the 100 fathom line is only about three kilometres from shore.

Hayward refused to believe they could be in waters shallow enough for a sounding to be taken, but at 10.20pm he agreed to slow to half-speed. At 10.30pm, when they still had not seen the Cuvier Light, Musgrove took another sounding. It read 95 fathoms and the tallow on the lead "had a deep impression which could only have come from a rock bottom".[7] The captain gave him the impression he did not think the line had actually touched the bottom. Musgrove asked once more whether they should turn around. Hayward said they risked damage on the decks if they turned in such a very heavy sea. But Musgrove's sense of urgency was having an effect – the captain instructed him to put the engines to slow speed. The mate warned the engine room and went back to the stern to take another sounding. It was immediately after this that the ship hit the island.

Crew appeared from everywhere. Much later, when a newspaper reporter asked if there had been any panic, one of them replied, "Oh no, but there was an urgent and widespread spirit of inquiry!"[8] They were ordered to their lifeboat positions but even a cursory look at the violence of the sea around them showed no boat could survive the mountainous rollers. At 11.11pm, wireless stations received the first SOS message: "S.S. *Wiltshire*, bound Panama to Auckland, ashore Barrier Reef. Heavy list to starboard. Sixteen feet [4.6 metres] of water in No. 1 hold. Danger imminent. Serious. She is listing more and more." For the next hour, the ship's wireless officers tapped out the deteriorating situation in morse:

Captain Bertram Hayward

The *Wiltshire*'s master had many years' experience at sea, but on the night of 31 May 1922 he made two significant errors in judgement.

"11.35pm – Send assistance at once. In great danger.
12.10am – *Wiltshire* advises captain says he is not sure, too dark to know, but thinks he is on the south end of Barrier Island.
12.26am – Nos. 1 and 2 holds are full of water. Ship very exposed to gale.
1.38am – Steamer badly on shore. Vessel rocking about heavily. Immediate assistance required to save life. Very thick weather. Ship on southern end of Great Barrier. Several steamers coming, but too far off."[9]

The telegraph messages were picked up not just in Auckland but also by a number of vessels at sea. The closest was the SS *Katoa*, a Union Steam Ship Company collier, bound from Auckland to Whangarei and about 4.8 kilometres south of Little Barrier Island when they picked up the first SOS. Captain J. Plowman ordered full speed for the bigger island but in the gale and heavy seas the lightly laden ship made slow progress, pitching and rolling. Much further off, the steamer *Arahura*, on its way from Auckland to Gisborne with 100 passengers, also turned and headed towards the *Wiltshire*. And at 5am on Thursday, the Auckland Harbour Board tug *Te Awhina* left Queen's Wharf carrying representatives of

Lloyd's and Customs, two policemen and two members of the press. The comparatively new medium of radio – called wireless then – had vastly improved communications. When the *Wiltshire* was wrecked, radio telegraph was used, ship to shore and ship to ship.

At 5.30am, the *Katoa* was directly opposite the Cuvier Light. "I sent up rockets and asked the '*WILTSHIRE*' if he could see them," Captain Plowman wrote in his report to the Union Steam Ship Company. "He replied that he could not. I then asked him to send up some so that I could locate his position but, of course, we could not see them as we discovered afterwards he was too far round the Cape for them to be visible from our position…. The sea was then so heavy that at times I hardly had sufficient way on to steer."[10]

The *Wiltshire* was across a reef in remote Rosalie Bay at the south-eastern end of Great Barrier. If it had hit the sheer cliff instead of the reef it would have slid back and sunk, and it is unlikely anyone would have survived. Great Barrier was another shipping "black spot" on the New Zealand coast. Wrecks and incidents of stranding dotted its shore line. One of the island's few settlers, Darby Ryan, described the vicinity of Rosalie Bay as particularly difficult and dangerous. The coast "consisted of high precipitous cliffs ranging from 200ft to 500ft in height [61 metres to 152 metres]. There was about 20 fathoms [36 metres] of water at the base, with practically no landing places. [It] was fully exposed to the violence of the easterly, north-easterly and south-easterly gales. There was always a heavy easterly sweep coming in, there being a strong ground swell even in calm weather. The situation was made worse by the strong currents racing round the end of the island."[11]

On the stranded ship, it quickly became impossible to use the rear decks. Great seas swept over the stern and up the main deck. Everyone knew the ship could not survive. The only question was how long would it last. All hands not needed amidships spent the night in the forward saloon lounge where the quartermaster on the piano and a steward on his mandolin played every tune they knew until the steward fell asleep and everyone else tried to do the same, while the ship shook and groaned with the force of the sea.

The next radio message was sent out at 4am and spoke optimistically of a chance to save the cargo "if the weather moderates". An hour later the mood changed:

> **"Fear ship will now be total wreck. Terrific sea. Our only hope of saving life is all to remain on board until the weather moderates, as no lifeboat could live. Will wire later."**

By nine on Thursday morning, the *Katoa* had confirmed the impossibility of a sea rescue when it radioed Auckland that it had left the larger vessel *Arahura* standing off about one and a half kilometres from the wreck and was moored at Tryphena out of the wind. Captain Plowman had sent a rescue party headed by his chief officer to make their way overland to the cliffs above the wreck. They took with them all the new rope on board the *Katoa* and a lot of stores. A number of settlers joined them. The party had an eight-kilometre hike to Rosalie Bay. At 10.15am, wireless operators picked up a brief message from the *Wiltshire*: "Position worse and desperate." It was to be the last.

SHIPWRECK

The stern section of the ship was now completely awash. An endless procession of waves broke over it and reared up from an army of rocks between ship and shore. "It was clear neither boat, raft nor human being could live in such a turmoil until the storm abated."[12] And the situation on the vessel was about to become much more perilous:

> "We suddenly heard, somewhere beneath us, an ominous crescendo of sound, then someone shouted, 'She's breaking up!' In seconds the more agile of us had tumbled or jumped down three ladders to the foredeck to await the Commander who, coming close behind, half fell among us from the bottom steps just as the terrible noise of rivets popping, steel plating tearing and woodwork splintering deafened us. We weren't a moment too soon for, as we scrambled to our feet and hurried forward to safety, we looked back to see the whole bridge structure, boat deck and funnel tearing itself free from the listing and waterlogged hull it had belonged to, rearing up, then swinging upright and tipping backwards. The first class dining saloon, now roofless, presented a sorry scene with all its chairs and equipment standing exposed. As we gained the forecastle we could see that the stern [section] of the ship with its fifth mast had broken from the mid section part we'd just left, and had disappeared into deep water. The waves, now battering the exposed end of the midship structure, began to telescope it into the forward section… accompanied by a continuing loud grinding noise…."

All food and water sank with the stern. While each of the crew was served a single biscuit, the sea around them rapidly filled with wreckage and spilled cargo – package cases of all sizes and their contents, mail bags from Panama, tins of cigarettes and cases of whisky. Two men volunteered to swim ashore but it was considered impossible – the water was far too rough.

The *Arahura* was still standing by "tossed in the huge seas… rolling so heavily that her bilge keel was visible".[13] They had watched the ship's back break with horror, the shouts of its crew heard above the storm. With the engine rooms flooded and the masts carried away, the *Wiltshire*'s wireless was now gone. The stranded crew sent messages by semaphore flags that were then transmitted on the *Arahura*'s wireless. In this way, Auckland received news that the crew were still alive. When the tug *Te Awhina* steamed into the bay, the *Arahura* and its 100 passengers continued on their voyage to Gisborne.

Those on the tug now studied the broken ship. "Several men clustered on the forecastle head, look-out bridge, and more were below…. Two lifeboats were visible in the davits on the starboard side, and a third had been smashed against the sides when lowered…. The tug was severely 'dusted' while lying in close, and the men on her had to hold on with both hands firmly to prevent them from being thrown about…. A waterfall on the cliff was being blown up like a geyser by the force of the gale…. Mountainous seas

THE AUCKLAND WEEKLY NEWS

With which is Incorporated "THE WEEKLY GRAPHIC AND NEW ZEALAND MAIL."

AUCKLAND, N.Z., THURSDAY, JUNE 8, 1922.

A STRIKING PHOTOGRAPH OF THE WRECKED STEAMER WILTSHIRE (12,160 TONS), OFF THE SOUTH-EAST COAST OF THE GREAT BARRIER ISLAND: THE TWO JUNIOR WIRELESS OPERATORS BEING HAULED ASHORE ON THE "BOATSWAIN'S CHAIR."

Wiltshire calling

Marconi's wireless telegraph was put to good use during the wrecking and rescue of the ship's crew. It also allowed reporters who sailed out with the rescue ships to send back up to the moment reports to their newspapers.

were setting in, and there was no possibility of giving assistance."[14] The tug left and moored alongside *Katoa* in Tryphena at 2pm; and at 5.30pm the *Moeraki* arrived in the bay with more reporters and a naval rescue party sent out by the USS Company.

The first rescue party from the *Katoa* had reached Rosalie Bay just after 3.30pm at the end of a hellish and exhausting tramp:

> "Incessant rain had swollen the creeks and flooded the roads. The rescuers waded the rushing torrents waist deep and climbed hundreds of feet of hills, slipping on the clay roads…. They followed the gully, splashing in the mud and water to the knees, and penetrated dense bush… laden with ropes, gear and stores, falling on banks, slipping on boulders in the creeks…. The last river was 10 yards wide and waist deep. By this time it was difficult to stand. All overcoats were useless and gum boots stuck in quagmires. The last stage was an hour's forging ahead in dense virgin scrub."

They found some of the island's residents already on the cliff helplessly watching the figures on the rocking bow 200 metres from shore, listening to their shouts as huge seas broke over it and flying spindrift reduced visibility to less than a kilometre. Some way had to be found to make a connection between ship and shore. While the *Katoa* radioed Auckland that the naval party with their rescue gear would not reach the bay until Friday morning, and the possibility of sending a plane was considered and rejected because of the weather, the men on the *Wiltshire* began trying to get a line ashore.

Time after time, lines fired from the ship or floated out tied to timber failed to come anywhere near. The five men from the *Katoa* climbed more than 30 metres down the almost vertical cliff face and scrambled out over the rocks to try to reach them, grabbing at any piece of wood that drifted close in case there was a line attached. They lay flat on the rocks, clinging on with their hands and feet as the waves tried to drag them off. At last, a line tied to a hatch cover floated near and was caught by the rocks. One of the *Katoa*'s sailors, Wilfred Kehoe, plunged into the surf, cut the rope and then, grasping it tightly, jumped back, with a wall of water towering over him, and clung to a boulder as it crashed over him. A great cheer of triumph went up from those trapped on the wreck. The lifeline was taken back up the cliff and a much heavier cable was pulled across and tied to a pohutukawa tree close to the cliff edge.

With a great deal of difficulty, they rigged up an endless pulley and then attached a boatswain's chair – "an affair like a child's swing, which would carry two people seated upon it, facing in opposite directions."[15] Four men were hauled ashore before dark, but it was hard work. There was no suitable pulley on the wreck and the rope sagged into the sea. Those straining on the land end of the rope had to watch their feet – they were on a muddy ledge sloping down to a precipice with only a tree branch as a barrier. Both groups spent a miserable night. Musgrove remembered, "It was nearing mid-winter, and this second night on the ship found us very cold and very wet." Above them the rescue party huddled together in pouring rain, chilled to the bone. "Three residents, one an old and sick man, came across the island late in the afternoon, and arrived in the darkness. They kept walking most of the night to keep warm."[16] In Auckland "people stood in the streets waiting for news."

Twelve more seamen from the wreck had been pulled to shore next morning before the naval party from the *Moeraki* arrived and brought fresh muscle to the task. With 10 men pulling on the "endless rope" they could bring across two men in 15 minutes. The navy team had also brought more supplies, and biscuits and cigarettes were sent over to the ravenous crew. They asked repeatedly for something to drink, but every time a billy of creek water was sent off, the jerking of the rope emptied the can before it reached the ship.

By midday, a naval pulley had been attached to the rig, landing times were speeded up and the sling of the boatswain's chair stayed clear of the waves. Once the crew reached shore, they were taken in groups back to Tryphena. For many, this final leg of the rescue was almost too much. They fell repeatedly on the greasy roads and while fording swollen rivers, ate even the crumbs of biscuits and "when they reached pools of muddy water in the fields… fell on their faces and lapped up the water".[17] They were met at the beach by one of the locals, Mrs Blackwell, who with the help of two little girls fed them an endless supply of hot tea and home-made scones with plum jam. On the *Katoa*, Captain Plowman was ready for the exhausted men: "… each batch were provided with a hot meal, had their clothes dried, and were sent down No.3 hatch (which was cleaned up and new canvas covers laid on the floor) to make room for others when they arrived."[18]

Back on the *Wiltshire*, the effort of the rescue was wearing down the dwindling number of men left. Musgrove was one of them:

> "We kept at it throughout the day, but the work slowed appreciably as the cable stretched; it took a long time to take up the slack, tired and weak as we all were. By nightfall, eight of us still remained aboard – but despite the difficulties of working in darkness we decided to carry on."[19]

Captain Hayward, although showing signs of complete exhaustion, wanted to be the last off his ship but his officers insisted he leave ahead of them as he would need help getting into the chair. They got the rotund man into the sling and tied him in; Fourth Officer J.G. Raven sat beside him. But while they were making the crossing, the captain collapsed, let go the rope, "slipped from the lashing and sank back, head downwards from the seat". Sixty metres below was the rocky beach. As they swung perilously about, Raven grabbed Hayward's coat and managed to sit across his legs, holding him until

Kehoe and friend
The hero of the rescue, 24-year-old Able Seaman Wilfred Kehoe, with the ship's cat which was finally taken off the wreck once the sea had calmed.

SHIPWRECK

they were pulled to safety. Musgrove and the chief engineer followed with some of the ship's papers in a canvas bag, the second-to-last pair off. With neither side able to see in the dark, and everyone tired by now, their journey took almost an hour:

> "It was a most unpleasant example of two feet forward and one foot back all the time, as the nearly all-in party on the cliff struggled with their herculean task. We rocked and spun with an unending succession of jerks…. For perhaps 15 minutes of this nightmare we were being washed around as the chair descended towards the boiling masses of water. Only by holding our breath and nearly bursting our lungs as each breaking wave temporarily submerged us, and gasping for dear life during the few moments before we were being swilled around again, did we survive this added ordeal by water."[20]

When the first and second officers were landed safely with the ship's log book about 10pm on 2 June, a full two days after hitting the island, the only living creature left on the *Wiltshire* was the ship's cat — the crew had thought it too risky to bring it over. A hundred men had been rescued from the wreck that day. The last 30 men off spent another cold, wet night in heavy rain, only partially warmed by a fire. At daybreak they faced the long walk back to Tryphena and the *Katoa* which would take them to Auckland.

Musgrove recalled it as a nightmare journey: "… we stumbled our way through miles of undergrowth, through swamps and streams, always in the rain. We began to move like men in a dream. I remember taking turns with the others in helping our commander, a thick set and heavy man, until later, by some stroke of good fortune, a man appeared leading a horse. We placed the commander on using a coil of rope as a saddle." When they reached Tryphena, they had been walking for six hours. The sun was shining as they were rowed out to the *Katoa*.

At noon the collier raised anchor and headed out of the bay towards Auckland. They arrived five hours later under a darkening sky in thick, drizzling rain to the cheers of the crowd waiting to see them. As they came alongside Queen's Wharf, one of the survivors called down, "What time do they close here, buddy?" "'Buddy' in the person of a stalwart constable, shouted back, 'Six o'clock.' 'Time enough,' replied the sailor, and the crowd roared."[21]

Fractured vessel
The abandoned and broken ship lies in now calm waters. Wreckage, cargo and mail bags washed up on beaches along the coast.

ATL G-16777-1/2 (Kinnear Collection)

Each man was given a package of new clothing and an advance on his wages after disembarking, and then driven to the Sailor's Home. The stowaway, an Irishman, George Murphy, was interviewed and said he had heard from friends in Liverpool what a splendid place New Zealand was, "but his short experience of it made him rather doubtful". Captain Hayward went to stay with Governor-General Jellicoe. The next day, the men were treated to a day at the races at Ellerslie and free seats at the opera that night.

Wilfred Kehoe was hailed as the hero of the rescue in risking his life to retrieve the line floated from the *Wiltshire*. The Union Steam Ship Company presented him with a silver tankard in thanks and he and the chief officer from the *Katoa*, who led the collier's rescue party, received £50 "in tangible recognition of the services rendered".[22] An extremely modest man, Kehoe said later, when he could be persuaded to talk about it, "The reason why I made a dash for [the line] was simply that I happened to be the nearest to it at the time. All the others would have done exactly the same if they had been nearest…. If [the wave] had got me on the first rock, I would have been gone, for the breakers were smashing timber to matchwood. I got to the second in time, however, and the wave had broken before it knocked me over. I seemed to go down between two rocks and then was lifted up again. That was all that happened." In fact his clothes were so badly torn that he had to do some rough and ready tailoring with bulrush the next day; and he was hospitalised on his return to Auckland for exposure, bruising, chest pain and pneumonia. He went on to become a well-known and much-liked ship's master.

At the nautical inquiry into the wrecking of the *Wiltshire*, Captain Bertram Hayward, commodore of the fleet of the New Zealand Shipping Company and the Federal Steam Navigation Company and master of the *Wiltshire* for a number of voyages prior to the wrecking, was found guilty of two errors of judgement: for continuing at full speed for nearly an hour after the Cuvier Island Light was not picked up at 10pm; and for failing to act on the result of a sounding an hour later. However, the court paid tribute to the conduct of the captain and his officers after the vessel struck. Hayward's master's certificate was returned to him but he was ordered to pay the costs of the inquiry. The ship was a total loss, as was over 10,000 tonnes of general cargo, although a few mail bags were recovered. Some of the cargo washed up on beaches along the coast from the wreck. For years after, those who went looking could find items from the *Wiltshire* in the sand.

Auckland Museum 13598

Sleeping in the sunshine
Exhausted crew from the *Wiltshire* sleep sprawled around the decks of the *Katoa* as it steams for Auckland.

The Treasure of the NIAGARA

Deep, deep on the ocean floor just 22 kilometres off Northland's Bream Head lies a shipwreck of great beauty. Six decades have passed since the RMS *Niagara* settled into its gloomy grave on 19 June 1940. However, it remains largely intact, lying on its side, the bustle of marine life around the promenade deck a ghostly reminder of the people who once busied themselves there.

The immense depth, 134 metres underwater, means divers have been unable as yet to penetrate the hull to unlock the *Niagara*'s secrets. Salvage expeditions of other sunken liners have recovered surprisingly well-preserved relics. To historians, the wreck of the *Niagara* is a veritable treasure chest — a time capsule of an era and a style of travel now in the distant past. But when the *Niagara* first went down, it was treasure of a far more literal kind that was on the minds of those in the know. Gold. Tons of it. Eight tons, or 590 bars to be precise, were secretly stored in the *Niagara*'s cargo hold. The story of the *Niagara* is as much about the salvage of that treasure as it is about its sinking.

When the *Niagara* was first laid down for the Union Company's Vancouver–Australia royal mail service in 1912, it was dubbed "The Titanic of the South Seas" — a name promptly dropped when a few weeks later the *Titanic* hit an iceberg and sank. But there was no doubting the *Niagara* was big — at 13,415 tons it was bigger than any ship that had been seen in the South Pacific — and it was certainly

RMS Niagara

Type:	steel triple-screw steamer
Built:	John Brown & Co Ltd, Clydebank, Scotland, 1913
Length:	160 metres (524 feet 7 inches)
Beam:	20.2 metres (66 feet 3 inches)
Depth:	10.5 metres (34 feet 5 inches)
Tonnage:	13,415 tons gross, 7582 tons net register
Engines:	12,500 horsepower. Two sets of 4-cylinder, triple-expansion engines and one low-pressure turbine, triple screw
Owner:	Canadian Australasian Line Ltd, 50% owned by Union Steam Ship Co of New Zealand, 50% by CPR Ltd, Canada; commissioned 1913 by Union Steam Ship Co of New Zealand
Port of registry:	London
Master/Commander:	Captain William Martin
Crew:	203
Passengers:	146
Cargo:	large cargo of small arms and eight tonnes of gold then worth an estimated £2.5 million
Destined voyage:	Auckland–Suva–Vancouver
Date of departure:	18 June 1940
Date of wreck:	19 June 1940
Location of wreck:	22km east of Bream Head, Pacific Ocean
Lives lost:	Nil

Cabin class travel

The first class dining room had all the glitter and style wealthy passengers expected.

luxurious. Photographs of life on board show that while the third-class cabins were little more than bunk rooms they still sported smart timber dressers, fancy rugs and vases of flowers. Of course the real luxury was reserved for the cabin (first) class areas: stately pillars, elegant fireplaces, fine furniture, handsome rugs and the very best silverware and crystal.

Its sinking in 1940 was not the first time the *Niagara* had hit the headlines in a negative context. In 1918, it had been blamed for bringing the great influenza epidemic to New Zealand. Just over two decades later, the *Niagara* was still on the seas and still highly regarded. As it embarked on what was to be its final voyage on 18 June 1940, the liner was carrying just 146 passengers – far outnumbered by the 203 crew – a reflection of the fact that only vital journeys were taking place in wartime. But it was not its human cargo that was of vital importance to the Allies. It was what the *Niagara* had in its cargo holds. One part of the top-secret cargo was half the New Zealand Army's small arms ammunition, which was bound eventually for England – a "mother country" under daily threat of invasion. Then there was the gold. In all, the *Niagara* was carrying £2,500,000 of Bank of England South African gold destined for the United States to pay for British arms purchases. As it sailed out of Auckland that afternoon, few people on board had any idea of the value of the *Niagara*'s cargo. Certainly, the German raider which had crept into the Pacific a few weeks earlier to lay mines across the entrance to the Hauraki Gulf had no way of knowing that its first victim in the Pacific would be such a dreadful blow to the Allies.

In both world wars, raiders operated like spies behind enemy lines, cleverly disguising themselves to look like friendly vessels. In the case of Raider No.36, known as the *Orion*, it had been disguised to resemble the Dutch trader *Beemsterijk*. Raiders were fast, heavily armed and their aim was simple: to disrupt and destroy Allied shipping in an effort to divert Allied naval fleets from Europe. The *Orion*, nicknamed The Black Raider by the prisoners of war on board, sailed from Germany on 6 April 1940, with Captain Kurt Weyher at the helm, making its way to the Atlantic through the Denmark Strait between Iceland and Greenland, and attacked its first victim in the mid-Atlantic.

On 19 May, the *Orion* rounded Cape Horn and entered the Pacific, arriving off the New Zealand coast on 13 June 1940. Weyher had an impressive artillery at his fingertips: six 5.9-inch guns capable of firing 100lb shells, a single 3-inch gun, six light anti-aircraft guns, six torpedo tubes in triple mountings, mines and even an Arado seaplane. But his priority upon arriving in New Zealand waters was laying the 228 mines he was carrying across the entrance to the Hauraki Gulf and New Zealand's busiest shipping lanes. Arriving in the late afternoon and with clear skies and good visibility at dusk, Weyher wasted no time.

The first barrage was laid across the eastern approach to the passage between Great Mercury Island and Cuvier Island, a second over the approach to Colville Channel and a third, much longer row, across the northern approaches to the Gulf. With the last of the mines dropped at 2.36am on 14 June, the raider steamed away to the north-east at full speed.

The weather was cool and clear as the *Niagara* steamed out of the Waitemata Harbour on 18 June. However, Captain William Martin must have felt some unease as he left the safety of the harbour. While there had been no evidence of German raiders in the Pacific to date, they had certainly made their presence felt in the Northern Hemisphere and they had made it to New Zealand waters in the previous war. What Martin did not realise was that he had already sailed through a minefield once – on his way into Auckland early that morning. As he headed back to the danger zone, his luck did not hold. At around 3.40am on 19 June, passing between Bream Head and Mokohinau Island, the *Niagara* struck and detonated a mine.

The Y-type mines used by the *Orion* were moored contact mines, secured just below the surface of the water to wire anchored to the ocean floor. From each mine protruded

RMS *Niagara*
Passengers on the final voyage of the Canadian–Australasian Royal Mail Line vessel included soldiers, businessmen, nurses, working men, women and children.

Passengers and crew all safe

The 349 survivors from the *Niagara* were returned to Auckland on the *Wanganella*. A clear night, calm seas, and the fact the liner's lighting remained on, helped in an orderly evacuation before the great ship slid beneath the waves.

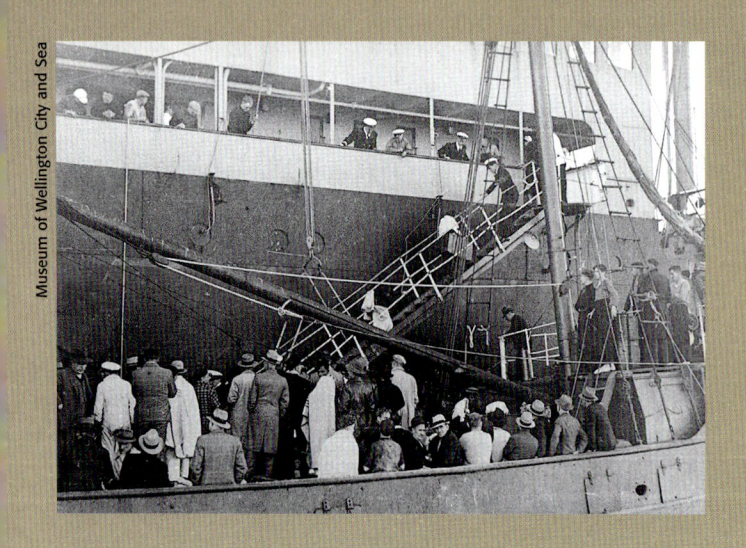

soft metal horns which contained fragile glass tubes holding sulphuric acid. When a ship hit a mine, the horns would bend, breaking the glass, allowing the acid to run to the bottom of the tube, triggering a tiny electric current which would in turn trigger the detonation of the high explosive amatol. The delay of perhaps one or two seconds between hit and detonation was deliberate. Ships usually hit mines with the bow, their strongest part. The delay ensured that as the ship moved the mine would slide along or under the ship where it could do far more damage. The *Niagara* was a textbook case of a mine doing its best work. With most of the passengers and crew asleep in their cabins, the violent explosion threw many from their bunks. Able Seaman Ray Nelson was one of them:

> "… It was dark, we had no light, so I groped around in the dark and found a pair of trousers. I got out of the cabin as fast as possible. There was a lot of confusion naturally. There was quite a lot of damage to the fo'ard part of the ship. The number two hold had taken the blast of the explosion. The deck in that area was splintered… I went to the bridge and Captain Martin sent me to try and find the ship's carpenter. One of his duties was to take soundings around the ship to see what sort of water we were carrying in the bilges… I found him down at the 'tween decks close to number two hold. He had already dropped the sounding rod… and he said, 'Jesus, the sounding rod has gone straight out through the bottom of the ship'…."[1]

Nelson rushed back to the bridge and was advised by the captain to get down into the forward accommodation and close the portholes. "… I got halfway down and suddenly I was up to my knees in water. I couldn't go any further. I reported that and by this time the ship was noticeably going down by the head and taking a list over to port. We'd done everything, like shutting the watertight doors along the bombed section. It was purely a question of was she going to stay afloat or was she going to sink?…"[2] Within a few minutes it was clear it was the latter. Martin gave the order to abandon ship, the radio operator broadcast distress messages and the crew started firing rockets to alert rescuers to their whereabouts. Luckily the passengers were able to make it into the 18 lifeboats without too much difficulty. The *New Zealand Herald* reported the following day:

> "… Wrapping coats around their night attire to ward off the chill of the early morning, passengers made their way in orderly fashion to boat stations. Wearing lifebelts and discarding any thoughts of luggage and other property, they took their places in a manner which prompted one experienced passenger to observe that it all went as smoothly as if it were boat drill… Even the ship's cat, spitting [his] contempt at disaster, was firmly grasped by a seaman and included in a boat's complement…."[3]

SHIPWRECK

However later reports listed the cat, Aussie, as the *Niagara*'s single casualty. "… not finding the lifeboat to his liking [he] scrambled back aboard the liner to go down with her…"[4] It was 5.32am as the 349 survivors watched the *Niagara* disappear to her watery grave. A nurse travelling as a passenger on the liner, Sister H. Munroe, wrote about her experiences:

> "The early morning was very dark, about 4.25am. The lifeboats were gradually drifting apart all around the stricken *Niagara*. The great old ship seemed to have steadied, and the hope of all was that she would survive. At the end of half an hour, the watertight bulkheads must have collapsed under the strain, for she slowly stood on end and slid under the surface. Sorrow was the predominant feeling for the passing of that fine old ship. We all felt we had lost a home. Even the men caught their breath as, like a great shadow in the night, she vanished from view. A member of the crew in our boat expressed all our feelings in the words, 'she's a grand old lady and she's dying gracefully, though she doesn't want to die'…."[5]

Amazingly there seems to have been little panic during the rescue – perhaps because the seas were calm and the liner's lights remained on throughout the ordeal. The rescue of the survivors was carried out later that day when the RNZAF's high-speed rescue launch arrived. Bigger ships on hand such as the *Wanganella* and *Achilles* kept a respectable distance because the *Niagara* clearly lay in the minefield, but the coaster *Kapiti* from Whangarei and boats from the *Achilles* helped pick up passengers and by 7pm all occupants of the 18 lifeboats were safely on land.

"… Women with dressing gowns over night attire, men with overcoats over pyjamas, the 350 persons from the lost liner trooped quietly through sympathetic lines of officials and friends in the customs shed…."[6]

"… A boy of nine or ten years stood out rather prominently among the rescued passengers by reason of the fact that he was fully dressed, even to his tie. 'When they said that the boat was going to sink,' he explained calmly to a questioner, 'I thought I had better put on all my clothes.' The matter of fact boy may be a quick dresser, but he certainly made himself thoroughly neat before he went on deck…"[7]

The loss of the *Niagara* came as a devastating wake-up call to New Zealanders that the war, once a distant horror, was now right on New Zealand's doorstep. Raiders were in our waters, minefields had been laid across our busiest sealanes. What was next? Our cities being bombed? Prime Minister Peter Fraser quickly issued a statement in Parliament appealing for calm and reassuring the public that minesweepers were on their way to the gulf.

> "… Members will, of course, realise that in this war, as in the last war, there is nothing to prevent an occasional raider from escaping the

network of patrols and embarking upon a career of surreptitious minelaying. It is, of course, highly regrettable that we should have lost this ship and her cargo, but there are at least three very reassuring aspects. The first is, of course, that so far as can be ascertained, at present there has been absolutely no loss of life. The second is that once the menace of a minefield is discovered it can be easily and quickly disposed of, and all necessary measures are… being taken to this end. The third is that it disposes of any suspicion that the loss of the *Niagara* might have been due to internal treachery…."[8]

Fraser may have been right about the absence of death or treachery, but he overestimated the ease with which a minefield could be destroyed. The remaining mines were to prove a terrifying hazard to the salvage team attempting to lift the gold from the *Niagara*. So begins the second part of the *Niagara*'s story.

A fortune in gold lay 134 metres underwater in the middle of a minefield at a time when the world was at war and enemy raiders were lurking. One might think, at a time like that, a salvage attempt would not be attempted. But that was not the view of the gold's owner, the Bank of England, which promptly asked the Commonwealth Bank of Australia to investigate the possibility of salvage. The man given the job was John Protheroe Williams, a successful Melbourne businessman who had made his money from stevedoring, gold-mining and engineering businesses. Appointed a captain in the Army during the war, he gladly dropped his post to take on the biggest challenge of his life. The diver he commissioned to assist was John Edward Johnstone. The agreement between Williams' salvage company and the Bank of England was meagre by the standard of the times when a salvage crew would often claim 50 per cent of the booty. Williams agreed to accept wages for himself and the crew and expenses of the salvage up to £30,000, plus, if the gold was recovered, 2.5 per cent of its value – at best a mere £62,500. However this was no ordinary commercial operation – the lads would also be doing it for king and country.

Williams and his crew, under the banner of the United Salvage Operations Pty, finally sailed out of the Waitemata Harbour on 9 December on their top-secret mission. But they were hardly surrounded in glory. Their salvage vessel was the *Claymore*, a derelict coastal steamer Williams had rebuilt for the task. During the first 160 kilometres of their journey north, her engines broke down four times.

The first major hurdle facing the salvage team, aside from the dilapidated state of their ship, was the minefield. Six months after the sinking of the *Niagara* and despite the assurances of the Navy, the mines in the gulf had still not been cleared. Minesweepers did clear an area of approximately a mile around where the *Niagara* was thought to lie, but

Souvenir

A ship's biscuit signed by some of the survivors from the *Niagara* makes an unusual souvenir.

when that area proved to be the wrong one, Williams doggedly ignored Navy orders to stay out of unswept waters and went further afield to find the wreck. Twenty days after leaving Auckland, the *Claymore* had its first terrifying brush with a mine – the very first time they tested the diving chamber. Having been successfully lowered to the seabed, John Johnstone noticed the bell had caught onto the mooring wire of a German mine. "… The bell was fastened to enough high explosive to blow me and the *Claymore* sky high if it exploded…" he later wrote. The only way Johnstone could hope to get clear was to be brought to the surface slowly in the hope the bell would somehow free itself. "… It was agony waiting. Hearing the wire scraping against the bell as it was raised, I peered out of my windows, waiting for disaster. Anyhow it would be a quick end. I would not even hear the explosion. I was watching the wire, hands over my ears in an instinctive if futile protection. I saw the dark bulk of the mine, the shackle where the wire was secured close to my face. The bell was rising, slowly, and then, scarcely daring to breathe, I saw the mine sway in front of me and drift away slowly. It passed downward, seeming huge and like some lazy, moving animal, then it was gone and I heard the cry, 'bell in sight' on my phones. I was sweating and shaking…."[9]

But the drama was not over. Two hours later, the mine wrapped around the *Claymore*'s anchor line. While the most obvious solution was to cut the anchor free, Williams did not want to lose the anchor and hundreds of metres of costly cable, wire and manilla rope. Attaching the anchor line to a floating buoy, the *Claymore* returned to Whangarei, advised the Navy it had found a mine and returned to the spot with the minesweeper HMNZS *Humphrey*.

Eventually the Navy and Williams' team devised a scheme where Johnstone would dive under the mine and attach a line from it to the minesweeper, which would then steam in the opposite direction to the *Claymore*, hopefully encouraging the mine to spring harmlessly to the surface where it could be flooded and sunk. However, as Johnstone went under the mine, his shot line wound itself between those delicate and lethal horns. As he came to the surface, the minesweeper suddenly moved and the mine flew towards him. Johnstone found himself jammed up against the hull of the *Claymore*, gripping none other than the detonating horns of the mine. For a few terrifying moments he froze until the cable finally slackened and the mine dropped, then shot to the surface by the whaleboat in which his support crew, including Williams, were watching aghast. One of the crew on board that boat, Arthur Bryant, later said: "… The mine plunged to the surface… it really leapt out of the water about three feet. I was standing quite close to it and for a split-second I turned away from Captain Williams, lost my breakfast and immediately turned back, wrapped my arms and one leg around the mine and was able to hold it without allowing it to rub the ship's side or bump the boat we were in. Whether I was there a minute or an hour I would have no idea…."[10]

Eventually, the mine's mooring line was cut and Williams decided to tow it to shore so the precious anchor and lines could be salvaged. Inexplicably, the crew and Navy ignored

Diving with mines

Deep sea diver John Johnstone in a traditional "hard hat" diving suit. He wrote later of the gold he had helped recover, "We took it from the deep blue sea, only for it to be put in a deep hole in the ground" – the vaults of Fort Knox in America.

his wishes and sunk the mine anyway, losing the anchor, cable and wires Johnstone and the others had risked their lives to free.

The second near-miss came on 13 January when a mine popped up just a few feet from the moving *Claymore*. "… It… slid, slid slowly along the side of the ship," recalled Ray Nelson. "You could hear it grating on the plates of the hull… everyone stood there mesmerised, not able to move. Just as well someone did. It was Arthur Bryant…."[11] Bryant had spotted the fact that the whaleboat was tied on the boat side in the direct path of the mine. He raced along the deck, leapt onto the whaleboat, untied its mooring rope and pushed it away from the *Claymore* with all the strength he could muster. A few seconds later, the mine passed harmlessly through the gap he had created. Two weeks later, on 31 January, the *Niagara* was finally found. It was now time to put the diving chamber to the test. Up to this point, diving below 60 metres was virtually unheard of. The only way to get a man lower was to use a solid chamber to protect his body from the immense water pressure. Air could neither be pumped to him nor could he get out to operate or move anything outside. But what he could do was use a telephone to tell those on the ship what he saw – in other words, act as the eyes for the people blindly operating the hooks and grabs to lay explosives and eventually start hauling in the gold. He could also breathe in this sealed environment by wearing a mask so his exhaled air could pass through a container of soda lime, which absorbed the carbon dioxide. By doing this, the diver could stay in the chamber for 10 hours.

However, there were some major problems. For a start, it was difficult to submerge, rendered semi-buoyant by the air which filled its ballasts, until the diver inside it could replace the air with sea water. The violent bouncing caused Johnstone to be so sick that he took to wearing gumboots in the chamber so he didn't have to slush about in his own vomit. Another problem was the difficulty in mooring the *Claymore*, whose movements would jerk and smash the chamber along the seabed to the point Johnstone started wearing a cycle crash helmet to protect his head from the inevitable smashing against the chamber walls. Eventually, the team devised a way to stop the chamber bouncing out of control on the sea floor – a simple counter-weight and rig so that whenever the ship rolled or moved the slack would be instantly picked up or wire instantly played out. But the factor no one could control was the weather. As winter grew closer, the swells grew larger and the weather rougher leading to many days when diving was impossible.

All of these problems meant it took three long months to blast through the ship's hull, through the stewards' room and across an open hallway where the strongroom was finally found in July. It was not until June, a year after the mines had been laid, that the Navy finally started clearing the minefield. Those explosions – many of them in close proximity to the *Claymore* – meant another disruption to operations. In all, 71 mines were disposed

Jeff Maynard

"Iron man"

Twelve years after the successful salvage operation, 60-year-old Johnstone returned to the *Niagara* as adviser to the second salvage expedition. He had been given the "rights" to salvage the gold. After many weeks, 30 more gold bars were recovered. The "iron man" suit, with Johnstone above, proved too dangerous at such depths.

of in the area in a single month. As Captain James Herd wrote to his wife:

"… We have undoubtedly been very fortunate to escape disaster as those [mines] now found are quite close to us, the last being a few hundred feet off and how we could have missed them after all the dragging around in the area I do not know…." [12]

When the bullion room was found at last, Williams informed the Commonwealth Bank of Australia in code and a former head teller was sent to witness the recovery. A *Sydney Morning Herald* journalist and American cinematographer followed closely behind, to record the top-secret mission. The bullion room was finally penetrated and the first box of gold hauled to the surface on 13 October.

Signed off

Postcards were among the luxury liner's souvenirs. The *Niagara* even had its own newspaper.

"…As it swung a few feet above the surface, spouting cascades of water, we saw that the spiked teeth had bitten into the corner of a mud-caked box and were holding it firmly between the grab and the apron underneath. 'By the gods. It's gold. It's true. It's really true. I can't believe it… Johnstone is that gold?' The captain could hardly trust himself to speak. He was very pale," *Herald* journalist James Taylor wrote. "'Not a doubt,' the diver assured him…." [13]

Finally, on 8 December, almost a year after salvage operations started, the *Claymore* hauled up the diving chamber for the last time with a staggering 94 per cent of the gold recovered – worth around £2,379,000. Using the diving bell, 316 descents had been made. The following evening it was party time on the *Claymore*. "… Ensign lowered three times in salute to the old *Niagara* over which we have laboured all these months, among mines, bad weather and hosts of problems that are associated with a salvage job such as this…" wrote Captain Herd. "It is with mixed feelings that we leave this job now that the time has come for us to depart… but we have achieved something and now look forward to returning to our homes…." [14]

On Monday 23 February, the *Sydney Morning Herald* ran the first of its scoops under the headline: "Bullion from *Niagara* – greatest feat of sea salvage." The 35 bars left on board did not stay there long. In 1953, a high-tech British salvage crew, with Johnstone as a consultant, recovered a further 30 bars. The other five probably remain with the wreck. It is anybody's guess when they may see the light of day again.

Niagara's treasure

The first box of gold was hauled to the surface on 13 October 1941, 16 months after the *Niagara* sank. The crew on the *Claymore* had good cause for celebration. Standing from left to right are: Tommy Nalder (with piano accordion), Billy Green, "Nipper" Lowe, Victor Neilley, Stan Mitchell, Bill Johnstone, Jim Kemp and Les Mischewski. Sitting from left to right are: Unknown, Ray Nelson, Astan Dianton, Danny Scott (partly obscured), James Herd, John Williams, John Johnstone (holding gold), Alf Warren, James Taylor, Arthur Bryant and Joe Alcock.

Museum of Wellington City and Sea

The Battle of the TURAKINA

On a midsummer's day in 1962, almost two decades after the end of the Second World War, a cracked and faded lifebuoy was delivered to the offices of the New Zealand Shipping Company in Leadenhall Street, London. Delivered with it was a letter from a retired German naval officer by the name of Kurt Weyher. It read:

"… After the fight between your cargo *Turakina* and my armed merchant raider *Orion* on 20th August 1940 in the Tasman Sea, we were able to save the surviving part of the brave crew. At the same time we did fish this only life-buoy. My crew handed over to me this life-buoy to remember a brave opponent, the brave master and his brilliant crew. Captain Laird was the underdog with his ship but did conduct the *Turakina* up to the shipwreck in such a way that we were full of admiration and appreciation. He died for his country while doing his duty.

"My crew and myself as former commanding officer of the *Orion* would like to express our respect to the survivors and the dead sailors in handing over this last life-buoy of the honourably sank cargo to your shipping company. Especially, we sailors are very glad in knowing that we are joined altogether in the NATO, and we hope that our efforts will be successful to keep freedom in peace…."[1]

SS Turakina

Type:	single-screw cargo steamer
Built:	William Hamilton & Co Ltd, Port Glasgow, 1923
Length:	140.4 metres (460 feet 5 inches)
Beam:	19.1 metres (62 feet 7 inches)
Depth:	10.7 metres (35 feet 2 inches)
Engines:	1196 horsepower
Tonnage:	8706 [8565] tons gross; 5429 [5373] tons net register
Port of registry:	Plymouth
Owner:	The New Zealand Shipping Company Ltd
Master/Commander:	Captain James B. Laird
Crew:	56*
Cargo:	4000 tonnes lead, wheat, dried fruit and wool
Destined voyage:	Sydney—Wellington
Date of departure:	18 August 1940
Date of wreck:	20 August 1940
Location of wreck:	260 miles west by north off Cape Egmont, Tasman Sea
Lives lost:	36

* There is some debate over the precise number of crew on board the *Turakina* and subsequent number of survivors and fatalities. Most reliable accounts agree that there were 20 survivors. However, even reliable accounts differ on the number of lives lost, with the official history of the Royal New Zealand Navy listing the total number of dead as 36, Charles Ingram's *New Zealand Shipwrecks* recording it as 35 and other accounts insisting 38 died that day. One clue to the precise number may be London's Tower Hill Monument, which lists the names of 36 men under the *Turakina*.

Museum of Wellington City and Sea

The *Turakina*

On 20 August 1940 the refrigerated freighter *Turakina* became the third New Zealand Shipping Company vessel of that name to be sunk by enemy vessels in wartime.

This remarkable gesture proved an honourable postscript to one of the great mysteries of New Zealand's war experience. It confirmed that the captain and crew on board the relatively defenceless *Turakina* had indeed put up a brave fight in hopeless circumstances, a fight which, for a few months at least, made New Zealand's sealanes safer for Allied ships in wartime. The sinking of the *Turakina* was another reminder for New Zealanders that the war was no longer a distant horror but right here on the nation's doorstep. In June 1940, the RMS *Niagara* had struck and exploded a mine off Bream Head and promptly sunk, thankfully without loss of life. The *Turakina*'s disappearance less than 500 kilometres off the Taranaki coast was further evidence that the German Navy, intent on disrupting and destroying Allied shipping and diverting Allied naval fleets from Europe, would go to the ends of the Earth to achieve its aim.

In the case of both the *Niagara* and the *Turakina*, the culprit was the same: a German raider, No.36, named the *Orion*. Disguised as a Dutch trader, the 7021-ton steamer was under the command of one Captain Kurt Weyher. Her unofficial name, coined by the prisoners of war on board, was The Black Raider. On a cold, squally late August day in 1940, the *Orion* was creeping southward in the Tasman Sea, looking for hapless merchant vessels along the much-travelled Wellington to Sydney route. Finally, late in the afternoon, she spotted her prey.

The *Turakina* was never going to be a match for the formidable raider. Essentially a floating refrigerator, the 8706-ton freighter carried a single 4.7-inch gun bolted to her stern which fired only 50lb shells. The *Orion*, although a converted merchantman, was a Goliath in comparison with six 5.9-inch guns capable of firing 100lb shells, a single 3-inch gun, six light anti-aircraft guns, six torpedo tubes in triple mountings, and even an Arado seaplane. (The 228 mines she had earlier been carrying had been laid across the entrance to the Hauraki Gulf.) Nor did the *Turakina* stand a chance of outrunning the raider as there was little difference in their top speed. A superstitious person might also say that fate was against the *Turakina*. She was the third New Zealand Shipping Company vessel by that name: the previous two had both been scuttled by enemy vessels in wartime. The first, a clipper ship, was sold to Norwegian interests and renamed the *Elida* before being sunk by a German submarine in 1917. The second, a passenger steamer, was torpedoed and sunk by a German U-boat in the same year off the English coast after disembarking a large contingent of New Zealand troops at Plymouth. As dusk fell on 20 August 1940, the third *Turakina* was about to meet her end in a hauntingly similar way.

The freighter was approaching the halfway mark of a journey which had started four months earlier when she left Liverpool in convoy under the command of Captain James "Jock" B. Laird. Her first stop was Baltimore, then Philadelphia and New York to load general cargo before heading to Australia, where she discharged at Brisbane, Sydney, Melbourne and Adelaide, loading 4000 tons of lead at Port Pirie, wheat and dried fruit at Melbourne and wool at Sydney. On 18 August, she left Sydney bound for Wellington where she was to top up her load with frozen meat bound for England. But two days later, 420 kilometres west by north off Cape Egmont, she was spotted by the *Orion*. Captain Weyher ordered full speed towards the *Turakina*, and, with the *Orion*'s powerful guns trained on her victim, signalled her to stop immediately and not use the wireless.

The German commander did not for a moment consider his opponent defenceless, noting in his book *The Black Raider*: "… That 'enemy' was the right word was indisputable; the ship's stern boasted a gun visible to all and she was identified at leisure during the approach manoeuvres."[2] His healthy respect for his lightly armed enemy was not misplaced. Laird was a determined man, who had vowed upon leaving Sydney that he would fight to the bitter end if challenged by a raider. His actions that day prove he was true to his word. In any case, even modest damage to the *Orion* thousands of miles from home in enemy-controlled seas could prove fatal. With his ship clearly outmatched and well within the *Orion*'s firing range, Laird chose to ignore the German command. Instead he ordered full speed, turned the freighter away from the raider and told his radio office to broadcast the "raider signal", the *Turakina*'s position and the fact she was under attack.

On board the *Orion*, the message came through from the radio room. "… Enemy signalling QQQ and position, about 260 miles north-west of Cape Egmont, and 400 miles from Wellington…"[3] Weyher immediately gave the "open fire" order and fired the starboard guns. His first aim was to wipe out the *Turakina*'s radio and aerials while his own radio operators were attempting to jam the *Turakina*'s signals. Weyher knew only too well that if his whereabouts became known by Allied warships, the hunter would

Captain James and Mrs Gwyneth Laird

The ship's master and his wife on the *Turakina* about a year before its final voyage. Before the freighter set out from Sydney, Captain Laird vowed to fight until the end if challenged by a German raider.

SHIPWRECK

inevitably become the hunted – but his attempts to silence the *Turakina*'s radio failed. "… There was no denying the persistence of the *Turakina*'s wireless operator," Weyher recorded. "He repeated his SOS. 'QQQ position 168 degrees 43 degrees.' *Turakina* gunned for eighteen minutes, under heavy fire, until it was acknowledged by Australian and New Zealand stations…."[4]

So began the first naval engagement ever fought in the Tasman Sea. It was sadly mismatched. Even in heavy seas and rain squalls, the *Turakina* could be seen clearly against the evening sky as a barrage of 100lb shells found their target. The *Turakina*'s gunners fired back doggedly but they were shooting blind because of the early loss of their rangefinder. One of the *Turakina*'s survivors, Mr A. Slater, a seventh engineer on only his second sea voyage, wrote of the battle.

> "… We were turning stern on to the raider as he fired a broadside at us and they all hit. One shell brought down the fore topmast with the lookout, one hit the bridge, one hit the galley just forward of the funnel, another burst in our quarters and yet another hit the cadets' house at the foot of the mainmast. Our rangefinder was wrecked and most of the telephones put out of action. The raider continued to fire rapidly, some shells going over, some falling short, but others hit us.
>
> "Our own gun, on orders from Captain Laird, had opened fire and I think we gave 'Jerry' quite a shock. They tried to blind our gun's crew by turning a searchlight on them. They had no sooner swept the deck with the beam and settled it on the gun than we fired and the Germans switched it off…."[5]

Captain Kurt Weyher

The *Orion*'s captain, German naval officer Kurt Weyher, was full of admiration for the way his opponent fought back, against heavy odds, right to the end.

The *Turakina* crew fired their single gun without pause, new gunners rushing forward to replace the wounded and dying, as their ship was struck blow after blow by the raider's superior fire power. Eventually the *Turakina*'s efforts paid off, when a shell hit the *Orion*'s after-deck, failing to damage the gun, but causing casualties among the gun's crew. But it was not enough to save the *Turakina*. In a little more than 15 minutes she was reduced to a blazing wreck and was sinking by the stern. More than half her crew had perished and others were wounded. "The vessel burns like a blazing torch," Weyher recorded in his log.[6] Recognising the situation was hopeless, Laird gave the order to abandon ship and the surviving crew courageously negotiated flames and rising water to help the wounded and dying get to the lifeboats. Two of the port lifeboats were wrecked but one of the starboard boats was able to get away from the ship with three officers and 11 hands, seven of them wounded. Mr Slater tells the story of one of the many heroes on the day, Mr Need, the fourth engineer, who helped another injured engineer up from the engine room and into the one remaining lifeboat. "… He could easily have got in himself, but instead, went away to look for other wounded people…."[7]

Even as his ship was going down, Laird was seen making his way down from the bridge through the flames on the main deck, gashes on his head and face, itching to

Kurt Weyher Collection/Elek Books

RNZN Museum

Raider No. 36

The *Orion* was the first German raider to operate in the Pacific during the Second World War. It was a fast general cargo vessel armed with guns and torpedo tubes, and a seaplane. All the raiders altered their appearance, often posing as innocent merchant vessels. By the time the *Orion* crossed paths with the *Turakina* it had radically altered its profile. Both the large double masts on the foredeck, one of the prominent features in the British Admiralty's description, were cut down and a dummy mast and its derrick were moved aft.

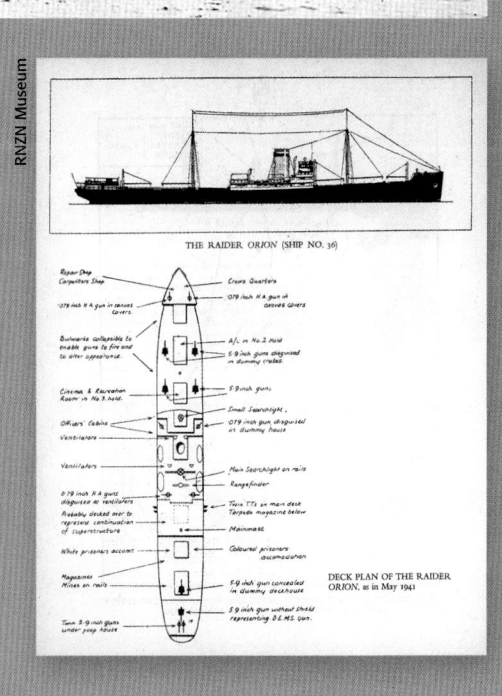

THE RAIDER ORION (SHIP NO. 36)

DECK PLAN OF THE RAIDER ORION, as in May 1941

"have another shot at the ———" but it was pointed out to him that only the muzzle of the gun was above water.[8] As the last remaining lifeboat was lowered into the rising sea, it swept away from the ship's side and it took some time to be brought back. That loss of time proved deadly. While the few survivors left on the ship prepared to leap onto the lifeboat and the order to jump ship was given, another torpedo found its mark: "… we got the chief radio officer into the [lifeboat] as it lifted to a sea," recalled Mr Slater. "Then four or five of us jumped together and someone caught hold of me as I landed on the boat's bows, otherwise I should have gone over the side. I looked up and saw the second engineer about to jump when there was a terrific flash and explosion. The next thing I remembered was thinking I was drowning. I had a terrific struggle to reach the surface. Then I looked round, but there was no *Turakina* – only wreckage was to be seen. We learned afterwards that the raider had fired two torpedos into the ship…."[9]

Weyher wrote: "The cruiser's gun was silent at last. The freighter drifted, a flaming hulk that sent smoke and sparks into the black skies. As the *Orion* approached to take off the crew, the *Turakina*'s gun suddenly opened fire again, at just over 3000 metres distance. Shells burst uncomfortably close. They were quite crazy. One unlucky hit in the *Orion*'s engine-room, and her fate was sealed. A few broadsides from the *Orion* were then poured in to break this desperate resistance, even the twin-barrelled 37-mm A.A. gun sent over tracer shells. Surely that ship, burning with an intensity that made it visible for 20 miles, would now vanish into the darkness of night?

"'A torpedo – to finish her off' came the command. But through the heavy swell, the torpedo failed to reach its proper depth and exploded at the stern without effect. A second raced towards the wreck. After the excitement of battle and the noise of the guns, the wind and the rush of the water seemed stilly [sic]; but suddenly this silence was broken by a terrific explosion, and the *Turakina* went down by the stern at 18:29, two hours after being sighted, a day's journey from the protective arms of Wellington Harbour…"[10] The *Turakina* sank within two minutes of the torpedo striking. Most of the deaths that day occurred when the first torpedo slammed into the lifeboat: the only survivors of the explosion were the third officer, the seventh refrigerating engineer, an apprentice, two able seamen, a fireman and a steward.

What took place next was extraordinary. Having taken the survivors of the only intact

Prison island

Three German raiders, the *Komet* (Raider No.45), *Orion* (Raider No.36) and their supply ship *Kulmerland*, anchored off Emirau Island in the Bismark Archipelago north of New Guinea. In late December, they put ashore nearly 500 prisoners, survivors of passenger and cargo vessels sunk in Pacific waters.

lifeboat on board as prisoners, the raider then proceeded to cruise back and forth amid the debris of the *Turakina*, picking up survivors who would otherwise doubtless have perished by daybreak in those wintry seas. This astonishingly risky rescue mission cost, according to Weyher's account, "five precious hours" and "60 miles that could have been put between her and the place of sinking". Weyher recounted a bizarre event which occurred after 20 survivors had been hauled aboard and the engines had been started to take the ship south.

> "… Then one of the watch heard a hoarse but feeble cry. The engines were at once stopped again, and every ear strained to catch a sound from the suspected quarter. The cry was real, but nothing could be seen in the pitch-black night. The *Orion* steamed slowly, somewhat to starboard, and throwing all caution to the winds, switched on the forward searchlight. Yes, there was another [survivor], struggling on a plank. The ship moved cautiously alongside. A lad of about seventeen years was hauled aboard. He looked around him and in fluent German with Viennese lilt demanded: 'Well, and where are all the hits? We were shooting very well.' Then he collapsed…."[11]

The boy was Taylor, a volunteer in the British Merchant Service who happened to speak German, who had swum in the "freezing, turbulent sea" for five and a half hours but still found the strength to give his German captors lip, demanding to know how much damage had been done by the *Turakina*'s gun.[12] In all, the raider picked up 21 survivors, but one of the able seamen who had been badly hurt when the *Turakina*'s foremast was shot down died shortly afterwards. Laird and 34 of his officers and men had died in the *Turakina*, leaving a total of 36 dead and 20 survivors, prisoners in German hands.

At last the *Orion* left the scene, still with six hours of dark remaining and the added cover of heavy seas, squalls and poor visibility. But Weyher was right to be nervous about sticking around too long after the battle. Within two and a half hours of receiving the *Turakina*'s distress signal, the only warship in New Zealand waters at the time, the HMS *Achilles*, sailed from Wellington at 25 knots. The one flying-boat available departed Auckland the following morning. The cruiser and the aircraft spent several fruitless days looking for any sign of wreckage. The HMAS *Perth* and Australian aircraft also patrolled the south-west Tasman in a bid to track down the raider, but their searches were equally

Freedom ship

The steamer *Nellore* was dispatched from Rabaul to Emirau Island to pick up over 300 prisoners, survivors of German raider attacks. They arrived safely at Townsville on 1 January 1941.

War limits coverage

War time censorship and fear of public panic kept news reports brief and light on information. Instead newspapers looked for and found human interest stories, like the ship's link with a Glasgow school. The children's decision to adopt it had been rewarded with cases of Australian ice-cream delivered by Captain Laird himself.

THE NEW ZEALAND HERALD, SATURDAY, AUG[UST]

(Auckland City Libraries A14385 - New Zealand Herald 24/8/1940)

Indeed, he was eminent among that rare body of toilers with brain who themselves are bridges; even as his career joined the nineteenth century to the next, his activity was devoted to making pure science the servant of applied science. So it came about, for instance, that his close study of a remote field of physics pioneered the achievements of wireless telegraphy and his grasp of higher mathematics enabled him to interpret Einstein's theory of relativity to an age wondering at first what it was all about. Educative work was to Sir Oliver, in many directions, a constant interest; by the publishing of popular books, no less than by the preparing of erudite papers for the learned to discuss, he was ever on the alert to drive a road for others' minds to use for their own exploring. As tutor at Bedford College for Women, assistant professor at University College (London), professor at University College (Liverpool), first principal of the new Birmingham University, he successively carried on such work, imparting a zeal for research as a worthy adventure. Famed chiefly as a widely gifted physicist, he will be remembered also for resolute quests, less adequately rewarded, concerning a material origin of life and the possibility of established communication with the dead. He firmly believed in a sure harmony between science and religion.

RAIDER AT LARGE

As with the loss of the Niagara by an enemy mine, the news that the Turakina was attacked by a raider last Tuesday in the Tasman Sea brings the reality of the war closer to New Zealand. How fortunately free this country has been so far from its major shocks and perils can best be realised by comparing the lot of its citizens with that of the people of the British Isles, the South of England in particular. However, the two communities have one thing in common; continued command of the sea is vital to the existence of both. That the evidence of enemy action in these waters should have been so small up to the present should be a reminder of the debt New Zealand owes the Royal Navy for the watch and ward it keeps. In spite of that vigilance, raiders are liable to escape occasionally into the outer seas. It happened in the last war, and was certain to happen, as it has, in this one. Actually, in re-establishing a navy, Germany was supposed to have concentrated on the idea of commerce raiding, by surface vessels as well as by submarines, rather than on any idea of fleet action. The small amount of success achieved so far says much for the effectiveness of British counter-measures. That does not mean that the enemy may not make other attempts to harry seaborne traffic, and even score some successes. He is resourceful, bold, and not burdened by scruples. New Zealand cannot rely on being forever exempt from the immediate consequences of war, and it is as well to realise the fact.

NOTES AND COMMENTS

LOCAL AND GENERAL

Prolific Lambing
In a flock of 650 Romney ewes on Mr. S. Given's farm at Pollok, Waiuku, are seven ewes each with triplet lambs and one with quadruplets, making a total of 25 lambs for the eight. All are thriving.

Compensation Court
The Compensation Court which is conducted by Mr. Justice O'Regan will sit on Monday morning to make fixtures for Auckland cases. About 30 claims are awaiting hearing, and these will occupy the Court for some weeks. The Judge arrived from the south yesterday morning.

Leave for Troops
A proportion of the troops at Papakura and Ngaruawahia camps were granted leave last night, and others will be given leave from noon to-day until midnight. To-morrow afternoon further leave will be granted a number of the troops, and relatives and friends will be permitted to visit the camps between 2.30 p.m. and 4.30 p.m.

First Battalion Training
Members of the First Battalion, Auckland Regiment, who have been going from their homes daily during the past two months for training at the Epsom trotting ground, will complete this section of their course next week. They will go into camp at the Epsom Show Grounds during September to complete their three months' training.

"Snakes and Ladders"
"We shall be having a snakes and ladders championship yet," remarked a member of the Taranaki Education Board when a teacher applied for two days' leave of absence to take part in table tennis at Wellington. The application was declined, the comment being made when it was remarked that leave of absence had been granted for football that "football was different."

Unusual Police Procedure
An unusual procedure was adopted in the Police Court yesterday, when the prosecutor stepped into the witness-box to give evidence. He was subjected to a rigorous cross-examination by counsel, after which the magistrate, Mr. C. R. Orr Walker, commented that it was unfair that a witness should also have to prosecute a case. "You are at a disadvantage, because you cannot re-examine yourself," he added.

Hamilton Anniversary
The 76th anniversary of the foundation of Hamilton falls to-day. Hamilton was founded by the members of the Fourth Waikato Regiment, who were recruited in Sydney during the Maori War by Captain William Steele as a body of militia, and who landed at Hamilton on August 24, 1864. The locality was then known as Kirikiriroa, and was renamed after Captain J. F. C. Hamilton, of H.M.S. Esk, who was killed at Gate Pa, Tauranga.

Operation After Game
To be able to play a good game of Rugby and be operated on within an hour for appendicitis was the experience of a Hastings boy, Sidney Reid, son of Mr. S. J. Reid, the well-known horse trainer, this week. Reid represented the Hastings primary schools in the Ross Shield Rugby tournament at Waipukurau, and following the match he became suddenly ill, and was rushed to a private hospital where he was operated on without delay. His condition is reported to be satisfactory.

A Thrifty Bird
A grey warbler at Titirangi has shown, in addition to commencing building operations at an unusually early...

NO FURTHER WORD

STEAMER TURAKINA

DUE LAST WEDNESDAY

NOT YET ARRIVED

MR. FRASER'S STATEMENT

[BY TELEGRAPH—SPECIAL REPORTER]
WELLINGTON, Friday

"The steamer Turakina, which reported on Tuesday evening that she was being attacked and gunned by a raider in the Tasman Sea, is now overdue at a New Zealand port," said the Prime Minister, the Rt. Hon. P. Fraser, in a statement issued late to-night.

"No further communication has been received from the Turakina," Mr. Fraser continued. "She was due at a New Zealand port on the evening of Wednesday, but has not arrived."

CREW OF SIXTY

OIL-BURNING VESSEL

THIRD SHIP OF SAME NAME

ONE TORPEDOED IN LAST WAR

The Turakina was commanded by Captain J. Laird, and had a crew of about 60. She last visited Auckland in July, 1939, and it is thought that her complement would have changed considerably since then.

One of the first oil-burners to visit New Zealand, the Turakina was built in 1923 at Glasgow, by W. Hamilton and Company, Limited, and was registered at Plymouth. She was 460ft. in length, with a tonnage of 8706, and was equipped with refrigerating machinery.

The Turakina is the third vessel in the United Kingdom trade to bear the name. The first was previously the ship City of Perth, which was driven ashore at Timaru in 1882, with the ship Benvenue. The latter struck broadside on and was a total loss, but the City of Perth hit the Benvenue end-on and was refloated and renamed. She made a reputation as a fast sailer, and on one trip overtook the steamer Ruapehu when the Ruapehu was travelling at 14½ knots.

The second vessel of the name was built in 1902 for passenger and cargo trade between New Zealand and the United Kingdom. In 1908 fire broke out in the cargo while she was at Wellington, but it was extinguished with the aid of the tug Terawhiti. This Turakina met her end on August 13, 1917, when she was torpedoed off Bishop Rock shortly after she had disembarked at Plymouth a portion of the 25th Reinforcements for the New Zealand Division.

VESSELS BARBOUND

FIVE SHIPS AT GREYMOUTH

SHOALING AND HEAVY SEAS

[BY TELEGRAPH—OWN CORRESPONDENT]
GREYMOUTH, Friday

Heavy seas on the bar to-day made shipping movements impracticable at Greymouth for the second day in succes[sion]...

RAIDER ATTACK

SHIP IN TASMAN

TURAKINA'S CALL

SEARCH FOR ENEMY

NAVY AND AIR FORCE

ALL POSSIBLE STEPS

(Auckland City Libraries A14386 - New Zealand Herald 23/8/1940)

[BY TELEGRAPH—SPECIAL REPORTER]
WELLINGTON, Thursday

An announcement that on Tuesday evening advice was received by wireless from the steamer Turakina in the Tasman Sea, that she was being attacked and gunned by a raider, was made to-night by the Prime Minister, the Rt. Hon. P. Fraser. The message was received at 6.28 p.m. on Tuesday, giving the latitude and longitude of the Turakina at the time.

"All possible steps were immediately taken by the New Zealand naval forces and the Royal New Zealand Air Force to locate and deal with the raider, and the search is continuing," the Prime Minister said. "No further information is at present available."

The Prime Minister explained that it had not been possible to make an earlier announcement, owing to the need of preserving secrecy, so that the effectiveness of the steps being taken should not be prejudiced.

The Turakina is a vessel of 8706 tons, and was built for the New Zealand Shipping Company, Limited, at Glasgow in 1923. She is 460ft. in length and is powered by steam turbines. The master is Captain P. Laird.

THE TURAKINA

LINK WITH SCHOOL

ADOPTED BY CHILDREN

INTEREST IN GLASGOW

(Auckland City Libraries A14382 - New Zealand Herald 22/8/1940)

When the brief announcement of an enemy raider's attack on the British steamer Turakina was flashed across the world, few could have received the news with a deeper or more personal anxiety than the pupils of a county school in Glasgow. The Turakina was the ship of their "adoption," and for years they have followed her voyages to distant seas as correspondents of her commander, Captain P. Laird.

A Glasgow man, Captain Laird adopted the children as they adopted him and his ship. Rarely was there a port of call at which a pile of letters addressed in unformed handwriting did not await the Turakina, and to these Captain Laird meticulously replied. His descriptions of life, trade and industry in distant lands provided vivid material for geography lessons, and friends in Auckland said yesterday that he had the gift of writing simple explanations. There was rarely a child's question that went unanswered.

Occasionally Captain Laird would visit the school. It was an almost riotous day for the children when he arrived during one English summer with cans of ice cream bought in Australia and carried to Glasgow in the refrigerated holds of his ship.

Prior to commanding the Turakina, Captain Laird was chief officer of the Ruapehu. His wife is a former New Zealander, but, with their five children, she now lives in Glasgow.

SINKING OF SHIP CLAIMED

A GERMAN STATEMENT

LONDON, August 25
The German High Command states: "Our sea forces sank the Turakina in Australian waters."

futile. In fact, Weyher had escaped to the south-west, and eventually made his way back to the Pacific to hunt further prey. His new prisoners of war were eventually transported back to Europe, bound for German concentration camps.

News soon broke in New Zealand that something was amiss with the *Turakina*. The Prime Minister, the Rt Hon Peter Fraser, issued a statement on 23 August, saying the *Turakina* had reported that she was under attack and was now overdue. Laird's wife, Gwyneth, who lived in Scotland with her five children, was on holiday with the family when she learned of the tragedy from the newspaper. She returned home to Brodic to find a telegram from Prime Minister Fraser:

> "… REGRET TURAKINA REPORTED HERSELF ATTACKED IN TASMAN BY RAIDER AND GUNNED STOP FEARED LOST OR CAPTURED STOP SHIPS COMPLEMENT PROBABLY PRISONERS."[13]

The telegram gave the family misplaced hope that Laird might have survived; it would be several months before the news emerged that he had perished in that second torpedo burst. Meanwhile, the attack on the *Turakina* threw New Zealand into turmoil. A *New Zealand Herald* editorial in the days following the *Turakina*'s loss reflected the unease:

> "… As with the loss of the *Niagara* by an enemy mine, the news that the *Turakina* was attacked by a raider last Tuesday in the Tasman Sea brings the reality of the war closer to New Zealand… That the evidence of enemy action in these waters should have been so small up to the present should be a reminder of the debt New Zealand owes to the Royal Navy for the watch and ward it keeps. In spite of that vigilance, raiders are liable to escape occasionally into the outer seas. It happened in the last war, and was certain to happen, as it has, in this one…. [The enemy] is resourceful, bold, and not burdened by scruples. New Zealand cannot rely on being forever exempt from the immediate consequences of war, and it is as well to realise the fact…."[14]

In the wake of the loss of the *Turakina* and *Niagara*, the Home Guard was established on these shores. Later still, after the loss of two more ships, the *Holmwood* and *Rangitane*, to German raiders, blackouts were introduced in Auckland. Suspicions were also rising that enemy raiders were somehow gaining access to critical intelligence about New Zealand's shipping movements. These were fuelled by the claims of the *Holmwood* commander, Captain James Miller, who was taken prisoner for a time aboard the raider that sank his ship. He reported that the German commander had bragged that spies on New Zealand shores kept him informed "of every ship leaving these shores and even knew the actual times that the vessels left port".[15] A shocked Prime Minister Fraser called for an inquiry and report from the Navy. Meanwhile, suspicion had escalated to paranoia, to the point the National Commercial Broadcasting

Service was accused of unwittingly broadcasting coded messages to the enemy via birthday greetings, advertisements and even the titles of music records.[16] However, when the Commission of Inquiry finally reported back, after hearing evidence from 31 survivors from sunken ships and 59 other witnesses, it found that German raiders did not appear to have had any inside information. Later accounts from the German commanders themselves appeared to support this finding.

Details of the *Turakina*'s fate remained sketchy for years. With tight restrictions on news media at the time, and all the survivors in enemy hands, no one knew exactly what had happened to the ship or whether there had been survivors. A single, dry sentence was printed in the *Herald* on 27 August 1940: "… The German High Command states: Our sea forces sank the *Turakina* in Australian waters…."[17] Weeks later, wreckage and large amounts of fuel oil started washing ashore in the north-west of the North Island, and when a young Dargaville boy found a piece of timber bearing the signal letters of the *Turakina* washed up on the beach, the *Turakina*'s demise was confirmed. Five long months passed after the sinking before the nation finally learned there had been survivors. The news came from a large group of prisoners of war rescued from the Pacific Island of Emirau where they had been marooned by an enemy raider. While none of the *Turakina*'s survivors were among those rescued, they had been told of the *Turakina*'s gallant fight by the German guards and believed there were survivors.

Over the next five years, details of the battle came in dribs and drabs. In 1943, two mess stewards off the *Turakina* escaped from a train en route to a German prisoner of war camp and their stories confirmed that the ship was sunk with torpedoes and the vow that Laird had made to "fight to the end" if his ship were attacked. But it was only after the war when most of the survivors had been released from German concentration camps and made their way home to tell their stories that the details finally came to light. S.D. Waters, who later recorded the official history of the New Zealand Navy, wrote in 1941: "… When the full story of the savage depredations of German commerce raiders in the south seas comes to be told, the very gallant action against great odds fought by the New Zealand Shipping Company's steamer *Turakina* will be revealed as outstanding in the annals of the British Merchant Navy."[18] Waters recalled a similarly brave battle of another New Zealand Company steamer, *Otaki*, in the First World War when "with just a little more luck" the *Otaki* might have sunk the German raider *Moewe*, scoring several hits, considerable damage and a serious fire on board the enemy ship. For his actions, Captain Bisset Smith was awarded a posthumous Victoria Cross. Certainly Laird's actions seemed no less brave.

In ignoring the German raider's warning to stop and not use the wireless, he carried out an obligation which had long been accepted by shipmasters throughout the British and Allied fleets. By continuing at full steam and transmitting the whereabouts of an

King's commendation

A commendation for bravery signed by Churchill on behalf of the king went some way to recognising Captain Laird's gallantry. However, there were those who argued he should have received a posthumous Victoria Cross for his brave fight that day which, with a little luck, could have sunk the *Orion*.

POWs return home
Prisoners of war rescued from Emirau Island brought home the first news of the fate of the *Turakina* and its survivors.

enemy ship, a captain might put himself, his crew and ship in grave danger, but the message would pinpoint the position of the enemy, and therefore potentially save other ships and help naval authorities. Laird, 35 of his men and his ship paid the ultimate price, but the *Orion* had to leave the Tasman Sea immediately and did not sink another ship for eight weeks. His determination to fight to the end was not misplaced. Two years later, a German raider was set on fire and sunk in the South Atlantic in a similar engagement. The Liberty ship under attack, the *Stephen Hopkins*, also sank, but her survivors had the satisfaction of seeing their enemy go down too.[19]

Strangely, Laird was awarded only a posthumous "commendation for brave conduct", and several of his crew awards for bravery and service – awards S.D. Waters described as "meagre"[20] compared to Captain Bisset Smith's Victoria Cross. Nevertheless, Laird's bravery is remembered in many ways, such as the letter from the German commander who ended his life and the testimonies of the ship's survivors. Perhaps the most touching salute, however, stands in Oamaru, where Laird was a familiar visitor. High above the coastal town, a stone cairn stands at Lookout Point above the harbour. The inscription on its bronze plaque reads:

> "In memory of Captain J. Laird, SS *Turakina*, who lost his life in action in the Tasman Sea August 20th, 1940. A GALLANT SEAMAN."

The Mystery of the HOLMGLEN

Sometimes ships are lost at sea and nobody knows why. They take the story of their last hours with them to their final resting place in the depths of the capricious ocean. The loss of the coaster *Holmglen* and all those on board has been one of New Zealand's most mysterious shipping disasters.

The *Holmglen* was one of a stable of coastal traders owned by the Holm Shipping Company. There were three others – the *Holmlea*, *Holmburn* and *Holmwood*. It was one of the newest of the group and easily the strongest and sturdiest. In fact, it was the strongest-built coaster in New Zealand in the late 1950s. The Holm Shipping Company's general manager, Captain John Holm, spoke with pride of the newest addition to the company's fleet. "She has been built exceptionally strong to withstand the most severe weather conditions that can be encountered in the far south," he said just before her arrival from Panama. The *Holmglen* had been specially strengthened to withstand ice and the severe weather of the sub-Antarctic seas. It would service the meteorological stations on Campbell Island and Raoul Island and from time to time carry Chatham Islands trade. By April 1956, it had begun work with the Holm Shipping fleet transporting goods up and down the New Zealand coast. During the next couple of years it developed a reputation as a "very lively" ship in rough seas, a "rock and roll ship", and difficult to keep on course in a following sea.

Peter Spinetto described a trip on the *Holmglen* from a passenger's perspective. When they hit bad weather "the

MV Holmglen

Type: steel motor vessel
Built: N.V. Bodewes, Martenshoek, the Netherlands, 1955-56
Length: 45.27 metres (148 feet 6 inches)
Width: 8.6 metres (28 feet 3 inches)
Depth: 3.04 metres (10 feet)
Tonnage: 485 tons gross, 219 tons net, 450 dead weight
Machinery: 6-cylinder diesel engine by Masch. Kiel A.G., 9 knots service speed
Owner: Holm Shipping Company, Wellington
Master: Captain Edward Joseph Eugene (Joe) Regnaud
Crew: 15
Cargo: 330 tonnes general cargo including flour, bran, pollard, wool, groceries, electric stoves and manufactured goods
Destined voyage: Dunedin–Wanganui
Date of departure: 23 November 1959
Date of wreck: 24 November 1959
Location of wreck: 35 kilometres east-south-east of Timaru
Lives lost: 15

Rod Donald Scrapbook

The MV *Holmglen*

The *Holmglen* is shown here as it arrives at Lyttelton for the first time in 1956. It was designed and built in Holland in 1955 during the worst winter since records began 250 years earlier. Two hundred ships, including icebreakers, became ice-bound in the North Sea. For six weeks the *Holmglen* was frozen to the side of a canal, and its completion was delayed because sub-zero temperatures made it impossible for welders to handle the steel plates.

poor *Holmglen* crashed head-on into big seas, coming to a complete halt at times....

> Meal time was something else. The dining table had its fiddle in place. This is a small railing to stop anything on the table sliding off. Also the tablecloth was wet to stop things sliding round, and everything was laid flat. You ate with one hand while the other held the plate."[1]

After the sinking, a wiper who had crewed on the ship recalled that the teapot from the mess-room regularly had to be recovered from his bunk. But for the men who sailed her she was generally considered a good ship "provided certain minor vices were attended to and she was properly handled".[2]

There was little out of the ordinary at the start of what would become the *Holmglen*'s last voyage. It had sailed from Dunedin at 9am on Monday 23 November 1959 with just over 300 tonnes of general cargo. Two men had signed off the ship after its arrival in Dunedin and replacements had signed on. But they were still missing a regular crew member. Bob Jenkins, the first mate, was newly married and had been on leave. He was due to sail down to Dunedin to rejoin the *Holmglen* on another vessel of the fleet, the *Holmlea*, but rain delayed its loading in Wellington. The arrangements were changed. He would join them at their next port of call, Oamaru.

The *Holmglen* took on additional cargo at the North Otago port the next day and it would stop once more, at Wellington, to pick up further cargo, before setting out for its final destination, Wanganui. After a delay in loading, Captain Edward "Joe" Regnaud and his crew were ready to sail mid-afternoon. A storm was forecast, but nothing out of the ordinary. The ship cast off at 3.45pm. Bob Jenkins was still delayed in Wellington. He would now rejoin them when they docked there. Captain Henry Williams, master of the tanker *Tanea*, saw the coaster sail. His vessel was due to depart later that day, but conditions in the harbour made it too difficult for the much larger *Tanea* to leave port.

The first intimation of trouble came that night. At 9.15pm, the Taiaroa Head lighthouse and radio station picked up a "mayday" call. It was the *Holmglen*. The operator on the ship's radio, believed to be Captain Regnaud, calmly gave the ship's name and its position – latitude 44 degrees 53 minutes south and longitude 171 degrees 37 minutes east. Suddenly the operator's voice rose. His next words were full of urgency:

> "Heeling hard to port... accommodation awash... crew attempting to launch boat...."[3]

Then there was silence. The operator at Taiaroa Head called back to the ship, but there was no reply. The distress signal was heard faintly at Wellington and Awarua near Invercargill by two of the country's three Post Office coastal radio stations. These kept a 24-hour monitor on the distress frequencies for coastal shipping. At Taiaroa Head, the operator picked up one more brief call from the ship – a request to stand by for further signals; then the radio went dead.

SHIPWRECK

While Taiaroa Head continued to call the *Holmglen*, the first moves in a well-established search and rescue routine were already in motion. The Wellington coastal station Radio ZLW began re-transmitting the distress call to all ships on both marine distress frequencies. The ship's position and details of the mayday call were also given to the police, navy, Marine Department, Wellington Harbour Board and the ship's owners. The re-broadcast "mayday" had also been picked up in Nelson. Captain Regnaud's wife always kept a marine radio on. This particular night she was at home making a Christmas cake when she heard the brief distress message come through.

At sea, ships off the New Zealand east coast began reporting back with their positions. At 9.40pm, the Timaru harbour master, Captain F.J. "Jack" Callan, received a phone call from Alan Glennie on watch at the Awarua Marine Radio Station. The harbour master immediately opened his home radio station. He arranged for repeated calls to try to establish contact with the *Holmglen* while he rang the police and the owners of four rugged fishing vessels, the *Norseman*, *Moray Rose*, *Seafarer* and *Craigewan*. From that point, he would direct search and rescue operations.

Of the ships at sea that had called in their positions, the closest to the co-ordinates given in the distress call was an overseas freighter, *Cape Ortegal*. The 6909-ton freighter was sailing south from Lyttelton and was 67 kilometres south of the *Holmglen*'s last known position. At 10pm, on instructions to assist from Wellington, the ship's master, Captain C.G. Mallett, turned the *Cape Ortegal* and headed north to search for the coaster. It was not an easy passage. The ship battled a heavy sea and winds of over 90kph. It reached the search area at 2am. "The *Holmglen* may have been drifting, so we swung to the north of the search area," Mallett reported later. He posted extra lookouts and had crew standing by the ship's boats as they circled. "We had no radio-telephone and could not keep in touch with the small ships searching. I don't know how the fishing boats stood up to the weather. We got quite a jolting round at times."[4]

Jack Callan had been quick to get vessels away to start the search. By 10.30pm, two naval survey launches, HMNZS *Tarapunga* and *Takapu*, had put to sea and reached the search area shortly after midnight. They immediately fired white and green flares and switched on search lights. The young skipper of the *Norseman*, Johnny Inkster, had been in the pub when he got a phone call from the police to say the *Holmglen* had gone down. He also set out on the search about 10.30pm. Mick Geddes, who was with him, remembers there was a real sense of urgency. The weather was terrible and it was pitch black, but "there was no question that we wouldn't go out… it was just a thing you did… there was a real mateship with fellows that worked on the sea".[5]

People came from all over town to help. At 11.30pm, two more boats from Timaru's fishing fleet, the *Seafarer* and *Moray Rose*, headed out of the harbour in conditions that would normally have made them turn back if they were only trawling. At 2am, the survey launch *Tarapunga* reported that conditions in the search area were deteriorating. It was unlikely any progress would be made before daylight. By the early hours of the morning, 17 more fishing vessels had joined the search – almost Timaru's entire fleet. A Japanese ship, the *Chowa Maru*, had been contacted by the Dunedin harbour master and was

Mike Regnaud

Captain Joe Regnaud

Captain Edward Joseph (Joe) Regnaud, master of the *Holmglen*, had previously been employed as both a harbourmaster and a sea captain, and two of his four children already had careers at sea. His death ended the family tradition – his youngest son had to find a job ashore.

expected around 4am. Another of the Holm Shipping fleet was off Akaroa when it received a radio message about the disaster. The *Holmburn* immediately set course for the *Holmglen*'s last known position, but it could only make seven knots because of the poor conditions. At 4.15am, it finally reached the area.

SHIP'S LOG – 25/11/59:
"At 0530 a large oil slick was observed in position 44° 36' S, 171° 34' E. Shortly afterwards a large piece of varnished woodwork was sighted.

"0700 Oil was observed coming to surface at windward limit of oil slick. Several runs were made to southward of this position using echo sounder and at 0730 an irregularity was observed on the seabed. Fishing vessel 'Rambler' asked to verify soundings.

"0800 Anchor buoy and rope passed to 'Rambler' to mark position. Naval survey launch also checking position...."[6]

The *Moray Rose* and *Craigewan*
Two of the first boats from the Timaru fishing fleet dispatched to look for the *Holmglen*. Almost the entire fleet was involved in extensive searches for the coaster and its crew.

The *Holmglen* had been found. It lay in 30 fathoms of water (55 metres) about 35 kilometres east-south-east of Timaru and roughly 10 kilometres north-east of the position given in its "mayday" call. In Wellington, first mate Bob Jenkins heard the news with disbelief. "I was home then and was going to the *Holmlea* that morning, and the phone rang at 7 o'clock and a friend of ours, her husband was at sea too, said, 'Where's Bob?' And my wife said, 'He's up in bed reading the paper.' And she said, 'Thank God for that. His ship's gone down and there's no survivors,' which is rather a lot to buy. I just didn't believe her. So we rang the office and they told us."[7]

The response of Captain Alex Grieve, the vessel's first master in New Zealand, was similar: "I was absolutely horrified because I had quite a few friends on board and it was a ship I never thought that would happen to. I know she was, they say 'under powered', but I really couldn't believe it when I got the news."[8] And in the shipping company's statement issued later that day, John Holm admitted, "I can give no explanation whatsoever for the disaster, but of all the ships in New Zealand likely to come to this end, I would have picked *Holmglen* as the least likely."[9]

The rescue operation in the radar room at the Timaru Harbour Board now concentrated on trying to find the missing crew. Those who had rushed to search hoped the crew had got safely off the ship and were heading for Timaru. The *Holmglen* carried two lifeboats, 10 lifebuoys and 27 lifejackets. However, the awful weather conditions would make it difficult to survive. Jack Callan organised an air search to augment the search at sea. It began at day break – three Devon aircraft of the Royal New Zealand

Sad return
The Nella with flag at half mast as it brings back the body of James McEwan to a waiting crowd at the wharf.

Air Force, the South Canterbury Aero Club's Cessna 172 and two aircraft from the US "Deep Freeze" squadrons based at Christchurch. He also made contact with two American aircraft, one a Dakota on its way to McMurdo Sound. The pilots signalled they had seen oil on the sea and a number of ships close by. The harbour master and his staff had been on watch since the search began, and were now in constant contact with over 20 vessels, plotting their deployment within the search area.

The fishing boat *Nella* sighted wreckage on its approach. The boat's skipper, Rod Donald, remembered "things floating, bags, oil drums, all sorts of stuff just floating, going up the line away from the boat of course. The hatches must have opened when she went down."[10] The wind had dropped but there were big swells coming up. The ships and fishing boats were all spread out "steaming up and down". The freighter and the coaster were three to four and a half metres higher than the smaller boats, making it easier for them to see across and into the peaks and troughs.

> **HOLMBURN – Ship's log:**
> "Resumed search. 0840 lifeboat rudder sighted and picked up. 0900 three life buoys lashed to a cargo tray with body attached – secured alongside ship. 0915 second body sighted in [kapok "fore and aft"] lifejacket. Launches 'Neillor' [sic] and 'Craigewan' called and asked to assist in recovering the bodies."[11]

The *Holmburn*'s added height made it difficult to retrieve the bodies from the water. In the running sea, they were reluctant to launch their lifeboats. "The *Holmburn* reported that she was four miles [6.43 kilometres] north of the wreck so we steamed up to her," Donald said later in his official statement. "We came upon a lot of debris floating, oil drums, bags, coir fenders, etc. and slowed our speed as these things were hard to spot in the freshening wind…. One of the crew, Alan Mervyn Gibbs, shouted to me to stop and on our port side we sighted a life-jacket with a body in it. On our second attempt we managed to secure the body with rope but the still freshening wind made it hard to avoid the boat rolling on it. The four of us managed to get the body on board and at that time the *Craigewan* arrived to pick up the other reported body."[12] Forty years later, the *Nella*'s skipper still remembers: "All he had on was a singlet and a life-jacket on over the top of it. Everything else was gone. Just lying face down in the water…. You wouldn't live in a sea like that, middle of the night, blowing half a gale. I s'pose they didn't have much chance really. No lifeboats gone or anything, you see. So they must have just went straight into the water."[13]

At 10am, Jack Callan ordered the fishing vessels back to port because of rising seas. Rod Donald remembers it was rough going home with the sea breaking over the bow all the way back. The last two fishing boats reached harbour at 2.30pm, just as the air search was abandoned because of the deteriorating weather and poor visibility. One and a half hours later, the *Holmburn* and the northbound intercolonial freighter *Korowai* were also recalled. The two bodies that had been found were identified as James McEwan, wiper, and Syd McKenzie, able seaman.

Twenty-four ships and launches and six aircraft had taken part in the search during that first night and day. Some, like Johnny Inkster and his crew on the *Norseman*, were 16 hours at sea. Over the next couple of days, two aircraft and boats from Timaru's fishing fleet continued to search for some trace of the 13 men still missing. The crews' eyes grew red and sore from staring intently out across deceptive seas. Many returned to port only to refuel and take on more provisions before setting out again. There was plenty of wreckage but no bodies.

Then on Friday 27 November, the motor vessel *Karu*, on its way from Timaru to Wellington, picked up the overturned lifeboat from the *Holmglen* just over 40 kilometres north-east of Timaru. It searched the area for some time but after finding nothing more returned with the lifeboat to Timaru. At dusk, police patrolling the beach between the Rangitata and Orari Rivers reported seeing two objects which appeared to be bodies. And the pilot of a Cessna on patrol a few miles off the coast just north of Timaru thought he saw a body floating, clothed in singlet and trousers. All these provided the impetus for one more concentrated attempt to find some answers or remains. The Minister of Marine, William Arthur Fox, ordered a full scale air-sea search for the next day.

On Saturday, three aircraft and 19 boats and ships covered nearly 2000 square kilometres off the Canterbury coast. The *Craigewan*'s crew set their course, put the boat on autopilot to free up everyone for the search, and kept an eight-hour vigil. A reporter on board described the searchers' departure: "The port was soon lost in the haze and, heaving slightly in the long swell, the *Craigewan* led out a long string of fishing boats.

SHIPWRECK

The boats dropped off one by one as they turned to begin the sweep to the north, and the *Craigewan* was left with the gulls for company."[14] On shore, patrols and fresh volunteers continued checking coast and beaches between Timaru and Banks Peninsula hoping to recover bodies. During the afternoon a ship from the Holm line, a naval launch and the *Craigewan* paused for a wreath-dropping ceremony during which all vessels taking part in the search were asked to observe a minute's silence:

> "It was a silent handful of men who saluted the crew of the *Holmglen*. The *Holmburn* hove-to above the wreck, with the *Tarapunga* in line astern and the *Craigewan* standing about 200 yards away. At 3.45 engines were cut and even the incessant crackle of the radio stilled as the crew of the *Holmburn* dropped 11 wreaths into the silent sea. The only movement for a few minutes was that of the waves. The *Tarapunga* and *Craigewan* then crept slowly past the bobbing floral tributes. By 4 o'clock when the *Holmburn* got under way again the wreaths – tributes from the Holm Shipping Company and its men, from next-of-kin, seamen's unions, and friends – had drifted out of sight."[15]

At 4.30pm, Jack Callan called an end to the air and sea search but asked the crews to maintain a lookout as they made their way back to port. A short time later, the *Norseman* spotted something in among a mass of wreckage about six kilometres south-east of where the *Karu* found the upturned lifeboat and some 28 kilometres off the mouth of the Orari River. At the coroner's inquest, Johnny Inkster told of the find: "At the time we received the message [to return to port] we were cruising in wreckage floating in the sea. I noticed a large flock of black birds sitting on the water amongst the wreckage. I made in that direction and found the body of a man floating in the water. The body had apparently been attacked by the seabirds. There was a life-jacket on the body in the normal position. After some difficulty we got the body on board the *Norseman* and brought it back to Timaru where we handed it to the police."[16]

Mick Geddes was also aboard the *Norseman*. "It was a terrible sight... the birds had done their job... you know... I just wanted to cut the life-jacket and let him go, but Johnny wanted to bring him ashore and do the proper thing."[17] A crowd of nearly 200 were waiting silently on the wharf for them when they tied up that evening and brought the body – no more than "near skeletal remains" – ashore. It was identified as Wilfred Harding, the ship's third engineer. It was the end of the intensive air and sea search. The *Norseman*'s crew joined some of the others involved on the naval launches and Geddes says they all drank rum till they were "nearly standing on their heads".

Although police and volunteers continued to search the shoreline for another week, no more bodies were ever found. The search had been the most concentrated organised in South Canterbury to that time. Many of the fishing boats had put in 40 hours at sea over the four days of the search. The harbour master had "hardly sat down to a meal" since he had received the mayday signal at 9.30 on Tuesday night, and had virtually lived

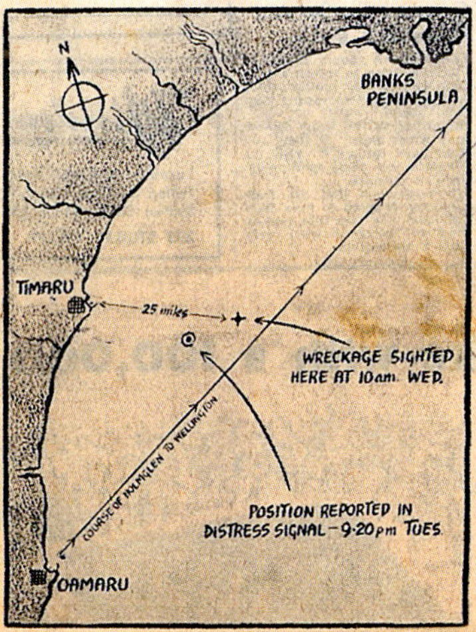

News of the *Holmglen*

News of the wreck filled the newspapers at the time. These articles were kept by Rod Donald, the captain of the fishing boat *Nella* that took part in the search.

NO SURVIVORS FO[R]

Tragic Wreck OF Holmglen

CAPTAIN E. J. REGNAUD  — **MR A. WOLGAST**

TIMARU (PA).—The full complement of 15 officers and crew is presumed to have perished when Holm and Company's coastal ship Holmglen foundered 22 miles east-south-east of Timaru on Tuesday night.

Yesterday morning the Holmglen was found in 30 fathoms of water, and searching vessels found two bodies, a considerable amount of wreckage, including part of a lifeboat and a large oil slick in the area.

The search was called off at 4 p.m. yesterday. In all, 24 launches and ships and about six aircraft took part.

The two bodies were identified last night. They were those of: JAMES McEWAN, next of kin, sister, Mrs M. A. B. Richards, 135 King street, Timaru, whose mother lives in Glasgow.

SYD McKENZIE, no address.

The wreck of the Holmglen, which was found by the Holmburn, a ship of the same company, using echo-sounding equipment, is lying about six miles north-east of where the Holmglen was believed to be at the time of her call for help. The position was also fixed by one of the naval survey launches in the search.

The Holmburn, plying at full steam for the estimated search area, ran into the oil slick about 5 a.m. She circled the spot—the slick had a diameter of about half a mile—for about an hour, and the crew saw heavy oil rising to the surface. Samples of the slick proved to be diesel oil of the type used by the Holmglen. Helped by the Rambler, a Timaru fishing boat, searching nearby, the Holmburn sounded the area, and established the position of the Holmglen. A buoy was dropped by the Rambler to mark the position.

About 8.15 a.m. the Holmburn encountered a collection of floating wreckage. There were cargo baskets, fenders, drums, dunnage, what appeared to have been deck cargo, and the rudder belonging to the starboard motorboat of the Holmglen. The rudder was taken on board.

Half an hour later the Holmburn sighted two bodies—one clothed in only a singlet and coat and supported by a lifebuoy attached to two other buoys. The second body was supported by a "fore and aft" life jacket.

Two Timaru fishing boats, the Nella and the Craigwean, recovered the bodies, which were brought back to Timaru about 1 p.m.

The Holmburn continued the search, steaming as far north-east of the scene as 30 miles, but no further sign was seen of either wreckage or the crew.

The two naval survey launches, Tarapunga and Takapau, which sped to the scene of the disaster at 10.15 p.m. on Tuesday, were followed within an hour or so by four fishing boats—the Norseman, Craigwean, Moray Rose and Seafarer. Other owners and skippers offered their services, and by early morning a total of 19 fishing boats were searching or steaming to the scene.

First reports indicated to the Timaru harbourmaster, Captain F. J. Callan, who is in charge of the rescue operations, that the weather in the search area was "not too bad," but subsequent reports showed that this was an understatement. The searching vessels encountered strong winds and high seas.

The overseas freighter Cape Ortegal, southbound from Lyttelton, joined the search about 1 a.m. and the Holmburn arrived about 5 a.m. The northbound intercolonial freighter Korowai also took part later in the day.

Because of the rising seas the Timaru fishing fleet was ordered to return to port at 10 a.m. The boats straggled back, the last two, the Norseman and the Seafarer, reaching the harbour about 2.30 p.m.

The search was maintained by the Holmburn and the Korowai, three Devon aircraft from the Royal New Zealand Air Force station, Wigram, the South Canterbury Aero Club's Cessna 172, and two aircraft from the United States "Deepfreeze" squadrons based at Christchurch airport.

Twist Of Fate For City Man

It was a queer twist of fate that Second Engineer Alexander J. Wolgast should be a crew member of the Holmglen, because Mr Wolgast (about 27) had saved more than a dozen people from the surf at St Kilda beach.

He was former captain of the St Kilda Surf Life-saving Club and had a fine record while on beach patrol.

He was the only son of Mrs Amelia Wolgast, 53 Caversham Valley road, who is in ill-health.

Mr Wolgast was an old boy of Caversham School and King Edward Technical College. He served his apprenticeship at Hillside Railway Workshops as a fitter, and worked for the Shell Oil Company before joining the Holm Line two or three years ago.

He was a crew member of the Holmlea when it ran aground about four miles outside the Otago Heads on November 10, 1957.

Mr Wolgast was a leading forward in the Southern Football Club's senior fifteen. He had played for the Metropolitan team and had been on the brink of Otago representative honours.

Chief Officer Keith D. Billinghurst (in his early 30's), of Grey street, Port Chalmers, came to New Zealand from England only about two years ago. Before that he had served for some time as second officer on Shaw Savill vessels.

He first lived in Dunedin, but moved to Port Chalmers on his marriage. He has a daughter less than a year old.

Two men, Messrs D. Renwick and Alan Iddon, signed off the crew of the Holmglen when she arrived in Dunedin. The present addresses of these men were not known last night.

They were replaced by two other seamen, David Weasterley (35), and Alfred Pemberton (30). Both are from Great Britain, but have been in New Zealand for many years.

Keith Lawdon Barker, who was second officer of the Holmglen, was first mate in the Holmburn at Lyttelton on May 7 when the master, Captain Derek Crabtree, and the chief steward, Alan John Hempstalk, lost their lives in a fire.

The master of the Holmglen, Captain E. J. Regnaud (58), who lived at Nelson with his wife, had an adult son at sea.

Captain Regnaud, who was born at Bombay, was harbourmaster at Motueka for 18 months about six and a-half years ago. Later he joined the Pearl Kasper Shipping Company and took over command of the Talisman. Before that he was master of the coaster Gael, and he also served on other ships with the Canterbury Shipping Company. For a short period he served with the Anchor Company of Nelson.

[Map: BANKS PENINSULA, TIMARU, 25 miles, WRECKAGE SIGHTED HERE AT 10 a.m. WED., POSITION REPORTED IN DISTRESS SIGNAL — 9.20 p.m. TUES., OAMARU]

No Survivors

Holmglen Boat Found Upturned

TIMARU (PA).—An overturned lifeboat from the coastal vessel Holmglen, which sank 22 miles east of Timaru on Tuesday night, was picked up about 7.30 last night by the 1,044-ton motor vessel Karu 26 miles north-east of Timaru. There were no occupants.

The Karu had left Timaru at 4 p.m. for Wellington.

The Timaru harbour master, Captain F. J. Callan, said last night the Karu would stay in the area and search. She would then return to Timaru with the lifeboat.

Three ships of the Holm fleet will meet this afternoon over the spot where the Holmglen foundered, and officers and men will pay a final tribute to the 15 who lost their lives on Tuesday night. The small buoy which bobs above the resting place of the Holmglen will be joined by wreaths dropped from the Holmburn, the Holmlea and the Holmwood.

The Holmburn, which sped south in response to the Mayday call from the Holmglen and later searched the area until late on Wednesday afternoon, will leave Timaru about midday. The managing-director of the Timaru Shipping Company, Captain J. F. Holm, has arranged for the Holmlea and the Holmwood to meet the Holmburn early in the afternoon.

Both the Holmlea and the Holmwood left Wellington yesterday for Dunedin. Their course will take them over the spot where the Holmglen sank.

The two members of the Holmglen's crew whose bodies were recovered on Wednesday, will be interred at the Timaru Cemetery this morning.

The coffins will be borne by representatives of the Timaru Fishermen's Association, the Timaru Harbour Board, the Royal New Zealand Navy, the Seamen's Union, the crews of the Holmburn and the Navua, the Timaru Waterside Workers' Union and the Holm Shipping Company and its Timaru agents.

Requiem Mass will be celebrated at the Church of the Sacred Heart at 8 a.m.

Captain F. J. Callan said yesterday that a conference of the Marine Department and the Air Sea Rescue Organisation had decided to discontinue the search. However, ships would still be in the area.

"Although this air-sea search has been discontinued, ships will still be in the area," Captain Callan said. "The search area is close to the normal shipping lane, and vessels approaching and leaving Timaru will keep a lookout. Local fishing boats also will assist."

The Timaru Harbour Board pilot launch Strathallan suffered a slight mishap when returning from the search area late on Thursday afternoon. The boat's water coolers broke down and the engine heated. She was towed by the Timaru fishing vessel Rambler, and temporary repairs were effected during the return to port.

Since Wednesday morning nine members of the Timaru Radio Club have been maintaining a radio link for the Temuka police between a base at Temuka and a mobile radio patrolling between the Seadown and Rangitata Rivers.

Sergeant L. P. Ricketts, of Temuka, who is in charge of search parties on the beach between the Rangitata River and Seaforth road, Seadown, said last night nothing from the Holmglen had been sighted. The search would continue today.

In a statement issued in Wellington, the managing director of the Holm Shipping Company, Captain J. F. Holm, said: "From information available to me, I do not believe there was anything unusual about the Holmglen's position at the time of the mishap.

"It is quite common for coastal ships to keep somewhat inshore from the direct tracks in the existing weather. The ship could easily have been making only seven knots or less. If there had been any trouble any length of time before the mishap, it seems certain that the ship would have reported earlier.

"I believe that the Holmglen could have withstood any freak wave that the Cape Ortegal could stand."

at the harbour radar and radio station. Volunteers had monitored marine radios, acted as auxiliary crews on fishing boats, or simply provided food for those in the search. But at its end, there was still no answer as to why the coaster had sunk. However, before the search was over, a full inquiry into the cause of *Holmglen*'s loss had been announced; and the Navy agreed to send down specially trained divers to inspect the wreck in the hope of discovering the reason it had foundered.

The dive took place over Christmas. A 27-kilogram camera was lowered with the divers. They found the wreck lying upright and on an even keel on a sandy and level seabed with the rudder hard to port. Scattered around it were bits of wreckage, tools, a saucepan and some books. There was no obvious damage that indicated the cause of the disaster. The Navy divers reported the vessel was intact, apart from a crushed guard rail, and there was no visible damage to the hull. Their only contribution to the mystery was to conclude that the ship must have sunk very quickly.

At the formal investigation into the loss of MV *Holmglen* there were nearly as many possible reasons given for the vessel's sinking as there were people called to give evidence. Frederick Parker, a marine surveyor and the first of 35 witnesses, said the ship had passed its last survey "with flying colours". His theory was that the vessel "broached to" – that is, the *Holmglen* had been broadside on to the waves and in a trough – and that judging from the wind it would have been held on a list with the possibility that its deck cargo had shifted. The coaster was permitted to carry 50 tonnes of cargo on its main deck and an entry in the ship's log book revealed that in May 1958, while crossing Cook Strait, a cargo of sacks of coal had broken loose in a gale and blocked the scuppers and wash ports. According to the second mate, the coaster shipped water over most of the well-deck when it was deep laden, but would normally shed the water quite quickly. Until it did, it would take on a slight list. In the May incident, it had been necessary to jettison some of the sacks to clear the wash ports on the port side and get rid of the water.

Eric Tutty, the foreman stevedore at Oamaru, told the inquiry that 27 tonnes of deck cargo had been loaded, stacked in tiers 1.8 to 2.1 metres high. He had noticed before it sailed that the coaster was "well up to the loading mark". Ken McCallum was loading that day. Forty years later, he also remembered that the ship was "loaded right to the gunnels, she was well loaded; in my opinion she was overloaded".

> "When we went to put the cargo on the steel decks, we laid dunnage fore and aft…. We put tarpaulins down and put all the cargo on that. We were about six or seven bags high. And of course they put tarps right over the top, lashed them down,… and when she hit a big sea, it is my idea that the cargo shifted and went over the side and just hung there like a big bag. It would just turn it right over. Course all the decks would fill up with bags of flour and all that sort of thing. There was no way she'd come right."[18]

Many others gave evidence that while the ship was not overloaded, the cargo was probably responsible for the coaster's sinking. David Renwick, an ex-crew member, recalled a voyage in heavy seas when the deck cargo – a tractor and drums – had shifted and the water had been waist high on the well-deck. The wash ports did not seem to drain the water away. Alex Grieve had taken command of the *Holmglen* when it first arrived from Holland. He thought that the "southerly bluster" which had blown up had "pushed up the sea very quickly behind the ship and… she was caught in between a couple of waves".

> "There were certain things that happened before she had sailed. She had taken a deck cargo of approximately [30] tonnes on the No.1 hatch and because she had to make arrangements either to discharge in Wellington or Wanganui, it meant the cargo was stowed on the forward end of the No.1 hatch. So [30] tonnes of deck cargo on a little ship like that, I would imagine, would make the ship a little unstable. I had the view that the cargo had shifted for it to turn over so quickly, and the vessel itself had very deep well decks. I believe when the cargo shifted in it, it was trapped into that well deck…. The captain said it was heeling hard to port, [which] gives me the view that she was caught in a very steep sea and probably broached with the swell behind her causing the cargo to shift, fall into the well deck and so give her a very heavy list. Water would then flow into the accommodation if there were doors open or ports open and the end would come very quickly." [19]

The Marine Department's chief surveyor, Victor Boivin, however, did not think the problem lay with the cargo. He believed that water entering the engine room, undetected or uncontrolled, rose until it caused the engine to stop, and then the generator, so the pump could no longer work. He imagined water rising on to the accommodation deck until it was awash. When the vessel foundered it would have been standing almost upright with its bows out of the water.

A number of witnesses felt sure the ship must have been taking in water somewhere. Johnny Inkster said the only thing that would make it sink so quickly was if one or more of the plates from its hull below the water line were lost, causing a massive leak. He thought the extreme winter weather conditions during its construction might have affected the strength of the welds. The ship's last survey had found the hull sound after new rivets had been put in a damaged plate. Bob Jenkins had sailed as first mate on the *Holmglen* for two and a half years. He knew the coaster well.

> "The first thing I thought of [when he heard the news] is 'she's got water aboard somewhere and she's broached',

Silent ceremony
Eleven wreaths dropped by the *Holmburn* into the water above where the *Holmglen* sank. The crews of naval launch *Tarapunga* and the fishing boat *Craigewan* joined the men of the *Holmburn* in observing a minute's silence.

which meant that she picked a heavy swell and she's swung broadside onto it… it's the only way the *Holmglen* could go with an outside force – too much water got into her somewhere. And it would have to be very sudden because a captain as experienced as Captain Regnaud would feel it in the ship…. The only puzzling thing with it is, he said, 'Heeling to port, and trying to launch the lifeboat.' If it went so quick, how would you have time to get a lifeboat out?… Normally if a ship went over slowly, you'd have plenty of time to talk on the radio. And Captain Regnaud was an experienced man and the radio was just behind the wheelhouse… so he had no distance to travel. If he had been worried at any time, he would have sent a message out saying 'I think there's something wrong' or 'We're starting to list'…. There's just something so violent. It's inexplicable to me…. If they were properly organised to launch the boat as in a drill, there would have been more bodies found…. My feeling is that it was so quick that no one had a chance to get out."[20]

The Navy divers had found the portholes open. This was presumed to account for "accommodation awash" in the distress message. But Bob Jenkins considered that as none of the crew would want to sleep with a wet bunk or water coming in, it could only refer to the portholes in the passenger cabins. Nevertheless, this would still let in enough water to affect her stability. However, he thought the water that swamped the coaster more probably gained entry another way. He recalled there had been a problem with one of the mast house watertight doors and six months before the *Holmglen* went down the handles had been taken off during repairs. They were put back upside down. This meant that heavy seas like the ones experienced that Tuesday night in November 1959 could have forced the lever down, opened the door and flooded the cargo hold. (It had happened on an earlier trip when Jenkins was on board.) He surmised that instead of flowing to the bilge where it would be pumped out, the sea water would have been absorbed by the flour and bran in the cargo. The coaster would quickly become top heavy with the sodden sacks and very unstable. This, he believed, was the cause of the disaster. He had asked for the handles to be refitted but to his knowledge the work was never done. However, an examination of the wreck during the making of the *Shipwreck* television series showed that both doors to the mast house door were still closed.

The official inquiry into the sinking of the *Holmglen* never reached a conclusion. But there was a general consensus that it had been a combination of circumstances. Counsel for the Holm Shipping Company summed up by saying the ship could not be presumed unseaworthy or overloaded if the weather alone had caused the ship to founder. The master and crew could not be faulted because there was no evidence the ship was overloaded. What could be inferred was that "for some cause unknown the vessel got across the sea, flooded, and then went to her doom. Any further inference would be pure speculation."[21]

"... Asked whether some disaster had struck suddenly or if some trouble had been developing for a long time, witness [Callan] said he favoured the latter view. The vessel was loaded to capacity, and with such a load a ship should rise upright. If it took a slight list it was inclined to ship heavy seas...."

CAPTAIN CALLAN'S VIEWS

Suddenness of Holmglen Sinking 'Indicates Instability'

P.A.   WELLINGTON, February 23.

Captain F. J. Callan, harbourmaster at Timaru, said today he favoured the view that "some trouble had been developing" with the Holmglen for some time. He also said that the suddenness of the sinking indicated instability.

Captain Callan was giving evidence on the second day of the Court of Inquiry into the loss of the Holmglen.

Asked by Mr L. G. Rose, for the Merchant Service Guild, if he had a theory as to what happened to the Holmglen, Captain Callan said the deck cargo was within safe limits and the vessel's seaworthiness well proved; yet the ship went over suddenly, which indicated instability. The radio message had said the accommodation was awash. That could have been caused by some of the ports breaking. Water running to one side could increase the list. The message from the Holmglen conveyed the implication that the ship was going to sink immediately.

Slight List

Asked whether some disaster had struck suddenly or if some trouble had been developing for a long time, witness said he favoured the latter view. The vessel was loaded to capacity, and with such a load a ship should rise upright. If it took a slight list it was inclined to ship heavy seas.

"I think she had a slight list. I cannot say from what cause," said Captain Callan.

To Mr D. W. Virtue, for the owners, Captain Callan repeated that he thought the Holmglen must have had a slight list.

Asked whether she could have made good speed to the point where the disaster occurred, as was obvious from the time she took to arrive there, if she had had a list, he said a list would not have affected her speed.

Search Detailed

Captain Callan said he received a message at 9.40 p.m. that the Holmglen was heeling and that accommodation was awash. He arranged for repeated calls to be made back to the Holmglen, rang the police and the owners of four rugged fishing vessels, the Norseman, Moray Rose, Seafarer, and Craigewan. The radioman reported no contact with the Holmglen and he radioed himself but received no reply.

He charted the position of the Holmglen and gave it to the masters of the H.M.N.Z.S. Tarapunga, the Craigewan and the Norseman, which left about 10.30 p.m., and told the other vessels to stand by in case he received further radio contact with the Holmglen. Other fishing vessels joined the search until 22 vessels were engaged, including H.M.N.Z.S. Takapu. He sent off the vessels he had been holding in reserve.

Captain Callan said Wigram advised that aeroplanes would take off at 2.30 a.m. A local aircraft began a search at daylight. The sister ship Holmburn was off Banks Peninsula and he advised her to make for the Holmglen's reported position.

His first message came in at 12.15 from the Tarapunga which reported it could see nothing, and the Takapu sent a message to the same effect. The harbourmaster at Dunedin reported he was diverting ships to the scene, and the Takapu reported it had seen a flare about 2 a.m. Several fishing vessels also reported seeing it.

Wreck Located

The Holmburn reported at 5.30 it had seen oil and established it was diesel. Oamaru reported it was sending out another vessel. About 8 a.m. two American aircraft, one on the way to McMurdo Sound, reported they were entering the air search and asked for instructions. They were directed to the oil patch. They soon reported they saw the patch, the Holmburn, and the fishing vessels. Soon the spot was identified where the oil was coming to the surface and a buoy was placed there. Echo sounders confirmed the presence of the Holmglen in 37 fathoms.

Oamaru advised the southerly was increasing, so he recalled the smaller boats. The wind increased and by 10 a.m. all boats had to call off the search.

Captain Callan said some of the boats brought back bodies which had been found. The Holmburn advised it would continue the search after dark.

Mr L. G. Rose, for the Merchant Service Guild, said it appeared that Captain Callan and all those associated with him had done a most meritorious job and he had been asked by his clients to thank him.

To Mr Rose, Captain Callan said the Holmglen had been found about eight miles to the north-east of the position given in its last message. That had not delayed the search. A flare would have been easily seen from the first position given. Early searchers had been over the position where the wreck was later found.

To another question, he said he would be in favour of some type of self-inflating life preservers in addition to present equipment. He agreed it was possible for one vessel's radar to interfere with another's, at a distance up to about two miles.

On liaison between search ships and aircraft, he said the ships and shore station had not been able to converse with the New Zealand aircraft, though they could with the American aeroplanes which were on the same frequency. Messages had to pass through Wigram by telephone. It would assist future searches if planes and boats had equipment of the same frequency.

Wing Commander John Donovan Robins, R.N.Z.A.F. director of signals, said that the radios in single-engined aircraft could not operate on the maritime frequency used by ships. Multi-engined aircraft were capable of receiving on this frequency but could not transmit. Equipment was now being modified to enable two-way communication between these aircraft and ships, and this should be completed in about four months.

'Bit of Mystery'

Lieutenant Commander George Brian White Johnson, R.N.Z.N., said he was in command of the naval survey launch Takapu which left Timaru at 10.30 p.m. to search for the Holmglen. At 12.30 a.m. the launch reached the Holmglen's reported position, which was about 18 miles off Timaru, but after searching the area they could find no trace of the vessel. About 1.59 a.m. he had sighted a green Verey light to the north-east and investigated without success. He later learned that none of the other search vessels had sent up the Verey light.

Mr Virtue informed the Court that the Holmglen had carried no Verey pistol or green cartridges. "This is a bit of a mystery," he added.

Captain F. J. Callan

Glossary of Nautical Terms

AB: able seaman, a man able to perform all the duties of a seaman aboard ship
abaft/aft: at or towards the stern or rear; behind
all plain sail: ordinary rig, fair sailing conditions
amidships: in or towards the middle of a ship
article: separate clause or provision in a formal document such as a contract
astern: at or towards the rear of a ship; behind a ship; backwards
ballast: weight carried low down in a vessel's bilge or on its keel to give it stability
ballast tank: usually called trimming tanks in surface vessels, used to correct or alter the trim of a ship by pumping water in and out as required
bar: raised area of mud, sand, stones, etc at the mouth of a harbour or river
barque: ship with three or more masts, all square rigged except the one nearest the stern which is fore-and-aft rigged
becket: an eye or loop of rope often slipped over the spokes of the ship's wheel instead of lashing it
bear/bore up: to sail closer to the wind
bearings: direction or position in relation to another point or to the points of a compass
bilge: bottom part of the hull of a boat or ship, esp. the lowest interior part
binnacle: case or stand containing a ship's compass, usually near the helm
blind roller: a long, usually non-breaking wave
boatswain: (also bo's'n, bosun) ship's petty officer or warrant officer in charge of certain gear such as rigging or anchors, whose duties include calling the crew and directing their work
boatswain's chair: plank suspended by ropes used to sway someone aloft for scraping or painting masts and treating rigging, yards, etc, or to paint a ship's hull
bow: front part of a ship or boat
bowsprit: large spar extending forward from the bow
broach: to be thrown broadside to a surf or heavy sea
brig: 1. two-masted sailing vessel with both masts square-rigged. 2. place on a ship for confining prisoners. 3. naval prison
brigantine: two-masted sailing vessel without square sails on the back mast
broadside: *n.* whole side of a boat or ship above the water line. *adv.* with the side turned; on the side; sideward
bulwarks: part of a ship's side above the deck
cable: heavy rope or chain used to moor a vessel; unit of measure equal to 608 feet (185 metres), $1/10$ of a nautical mile
capstan: mechanism with a vertical spindle rotated manually or by motor to wind up rope or cable, eg, in raising an anchor
capstan bar: one of the levers used to turn a capstan
collier: ship for transporting coal; one of its crew
compass point: a division of the compass card, the 32nd part of a circle, ie 11°
corvette: sailing warship, smaller than a frigate with one tier of guns or, in modern times, a small frigate-type ship of around 1000 tons
coxswain: person who steers a boat and has charge of the crew
crow's nest: platform for a lookout, fixed to the top of a ship's mast
cutter: single-masted sailboat similar to a sloop but with its mast nearer the centre of the boat
davit: one of a pair of curved or moveable arms, or a small crane, used especially for carrying a small boat or lifeboat, or to raise and lower it into and out of the water
dead reckoning: calculation of the present position of a boat, ship or aircraft without astronomical observations, by using the records of its speed and last known position and the compass readings of the course steered
draught: depth of water it takes to float a vessel
drift: 1. deviation of a ship (aircraft or missile) from its course, due esp. to water or air currents. 2. act of being driven along by currents of water or air. 3. rate or direction of movement or drifting, esp. of a current of water
dunnage: any loose material packed around a cargo to protect it from damage during shipping
ebb tide: falling or outgoing tide
fall: apparatus used for hoisting esp. that part, eg a rope, which is pulled on to raise the object
flood tide: rising or incoming tide
fluke: either of the two flat triangular pieces on an anchor that catch in the sea bottom
following sea: waves moving in the same direction as the ship
fore-and-aft: from bow to stern; lying in the direction of a ship's length
fore-and-aft rigged: fitted with fore-and-aft sails set from bow to stern
forecastle: the bow section of a ship, once the crew's quarters; a ship's upper deck forward of the foremast
foremast: mast closest to the bow of a ship
forepeak: the extreme end of the forehold in the angle of the bows
foretop: platform at the top of the foremast
forward: in or toward the front
futtock rigging: the short shrouds which give support to the top on a lower mast
gig: long light ship's boat, powered by oars, sails or a motor
gunnel/gunwale: the upper edge of a ship's side
hawser: thick rope or cable for tying up a ship
head: bow, or front part of a ship; also a term for a toilet
heave/hove to: to stop a ship at sea
helm: wheel, tiller or mechanism for steering a ship
HMS: His (Her) Majesty's Ship
hold: place where cargo is stored in ships
housing: part of the mast below the decks
hull: the frame of a ship; the floating body of a ship, excluding the masts, sails and rigging
inset: a channel, a place where water flows in
jib: small three-cornered sail
jibboom: spar that extends out from the bow sprit that a jib can be attached to
jolly boat: small general purpose boat carried on a ship
kedge: to move a boat or ship by pulling on a rope attached to a small anchor dropped some distance away
kedge anchor: small anchor used in kedging
keel: timber or metal strut running from stem to stern along the base of a ship from which the hull is built up
knot: measurement of distance and speed at sea: 1 knot = 1 nautical mile per hour; 1 knot is approximately 1.15 miles (1.7km)
latitude: any of a series of imaginary circles drawn around the Earth parallel to the Equator. All points along the Equator have a latitude of 0°, and the distance between the Equator and the two poles is divided into 90° of latitude, ie North Pole is 90°N and the South Pole 90°S. Latitude is used with longitude to specify any position on the Earth's surface
lead: weight on a measure-marked line used for taking soundings to measure the depth of the water, often coated in wax to get an impression of the sea bed, eg sandy, rocky, etc
lee: 1. side or part of a ship sheltered or turned away from the wind. 2. direction toward which the wind is blowing

leeward: side or direction toward which the wind is blowing
list: to lean over to one side
Lloyd's: old established English company specialising in ship classification and marine insurance – most ships in the world are insured with Lloyd's
log, log-book: book containing a record of a voyage or cruise
longitude: distance on the Earth's surface divided by imaginary lines from the North to South Pole measured in degrees. All points on the prime meridian passing through Greenwich, UK, have a longitude of 0°, and the distance East or West of this is equally divided into 180° of longitude. Longitude is used with latitude to specify any position on the Earth's surface
mainmast: the principal mast on a vessel, usually the second mast from the bow (in a schooner or brigantine); or the mast closest to the bow (in a ketch or yawl)
maintop: platform at the head of the lower section of a mainmast
make/made: to achieve or do, as in make sail, make fast, make alongside, etc
martingale: brace that supports the jib boom; or, a small spar that projects down from the end of the bowsprit
midship: of, relating to, or situated in or near the middle of a ship
midships: amidships, in or towards the middle of a ship, either halfway between the bow and stern or between the sides
mizzen-mast: mast nearest the stern of a ship with two or three masts; third mast from the bow of a ship with more than three masts
MV: motor vessel
neap tide: tide at 1st and 3rd quarters of the moon when there is least difference in the levels of high and low tide
patent anchor: a general term for a stockless anchor
pinnace: a small boat, usually a schooner, rigged with two masts; any of various ship's boats
pig iron: iron from which impurities have been removed in a blast furnace, used to make commercial iron or steel
point: v. to sail close to the wind. n. one of 32 marks showing direction on a compass card, the interval between any two such marks equal to 11 degrees 15 minutes
pollard: bran sifted from flour; finer grade of bran containing some flour
poop, poop deck: short deck above the main deck at the stern of a ship, often forming the roof of a cabin

port: left side of boat or ship when facing forward; to turn a boat or ship to the left. 2. porthole; covering for a porthole
preventer: line used for additional safety or security, or to keep something from falling over
quartermaster: petty officer in charge of navigation and signals
reef: n. part of a sail which can be folded in during rough weather or let out in calm, varying the amount of sail exposed to the wind; v. to reduce the area of sail exposed to the wind; so, close reefed – tightly folded sail with only a small area to catch the wind; double-reefed – to tie down a second reef in a sail
rigging: all the lines of a ship – ropes, chains and wires – used for supporting the masts or working the sails
RMS: Royal Mail Ship
roadstead: protected area near the shore where ships can anchor, less sheltered than a harbour
schooner: fore-and-aft-rigged ship with two or more masts, the mainmast as tall or taller than the foremast
screw: propeller
scupper: hole in the side of a ship that lets water drain off the deck
set: direction or course of a current or wind
sextant: instrument like a small telescope mounted on a graded metal arc used mainly in navigation for measuring the height of the sun or a star above the horizon to establish the position of the observer, and so the distance travelled
ship: sailing vessel with three or more masts; any large seagoing vessel
shroud: rope or wire giving lateral support to a mast on a boat or ship
sound: measure depth of water by letting down a calibrated line marked off in fathoms with a weight on the end, or by echoing sound off the bottom
soundings: place where the water is shallow enough to allow a sounding line to reach the bottom
spar: vertical or horizontal pole supporting or extending a ship's sail
square-rigged: having square sails as the principal sails
SS: steam ship
stanchion: upright pillar or bar used as a support
stand: to hold a specified course, take a direction
starboard: right side of boat or ship when facing forward; to turn a boat or ship to the right
stay: strong rope, usually of wire today, used to support a mast on a boat or ship; prow/head turned to windward in order to tack

stays: to miss or lose stays; to fail in attempt to go about
staysail: sail, usually triangular, attached to a stay
stem: bow of a ship
stern: rear of a ship
strand: v. to drive or run a boat or ship aground; n. land bordering a body of water, shore or beach
supercargo: officer on a merchant ship in charge of the cargo and commercial transactions of the voyage
tack: to beat or work to windward in a zigzag manner, close-hauled first on one tack, then on the other
top: platform around the head of a lower mast of a ship, used as a place to stand on and to extend the rigging of the topmast
topmast: the second mast usually directly above the lower mast
topsail: square sail set across the topmast
trough: long narrow hollow or depression between two ocean waves
trysail: a small strong fore-and-aft sail used in a storm
TSS: turbine steam ship
underwriter: person or company in the insurance business
unship: remove from proper place or position
wash port: used for draining away water
way: progress of a ship or boat through the water, rate of progress; impetus gained by a vessel in motion
wear/wore: 1. *verb, intr* – to come round on the other tack by turning the head away from the wind; opposed to "tack" often used with round. 2. *trans* – to put a vessel about, bringing its stern to windward
well: compartment in a ship's hold that encloses and protects the pumps
well deck: low-lying deck between higher structures that gathered water; in traditional "three island" merchant ships with three raised "islands" – the forecastle, midships bridge structure and raised poop aft – the well decks were the lower-lying main deck spaces between these "islands"; smaller ships might have just one forward well deck
whaleboat: long narrow rowboat sharp at both ends, once used for whaling, now used as a lifeboat on big passenger steamers and warships
windlass: drum-shaped axle round which a rope or chain is wound for hauling or hoisting weights, such as the anchor
wiper: a member of the engineering crew
yard: long rod, tapered towards the ends, fastened across a mast and used to support a sail.

References

BOYD
[1] P. Gidley King, in *Between Worlds: Early Exchanges Between Maori & European 1773-1815*, A. Salmond, Penguin, 1992, p349.
[2] *The Letters & Journals of Samuel Marsden 1765-1838*, ed. J.R. Elder, Coulls Somerville Wilkie & A.H. Reed, p59.
[3] Salmond, p351.
[4] King, in J. Lee, *I Have Named It the Bay of Islands*, Hodder & Stoughton, 1983, p38.
[5] S. Marsden in W. Doak, *The Burning of the 'Boyd': A Saga of Culture Clash*, Hodder & Stoughton, pp132-3.
[6] J. Elder, in Salmond, p369.
[7] J. Gordon in Salmond, p368.
[8] Salmond, p368.
[9] Ibid, p369.
[10] A. Berry in O. Wilson, *Kororareka & Other Essays*, John McIndoe Ltd, 1990, p19.
[11] Berry in Salmond, p374.
[12] Berry in Doak, pp72-3.
[13] Ibid, p79.
[14] B. Biggs, In the Beginning, *The Oxford Illustrated History of New Zealand*, ed. K. Sinclair, Oxford University Press, 1993, p18.
[15] Sherrin, *The Early History of New Zealand*, H. Brett, 1890, p152.
[16] Ibid.
[17] Ibid, p153.
[18] Ibid, p154.
[19] Ibid, p147.
[20] Wilson, p24.
[21] Salmond, p388.
[22] In Wilson, p25.
[23] Nicholas, in Sherrin, p150.
[24] Ibid.
[25] T. Simpson, *Art & Massacre: Documentary Racism in The Burning of the Boyd*, The Cultural Construction Co. 1993, p8.
[26] R. Cruise in Doak, p148.

ORPHEUS
Although other books have been written about the *Orpheus*, Thayer Fairburn's *The Orpheus Disaster* is considered the most authoritative.
[1] T. Fairburn, *The Orpheus Disaster*, Whakatane & District Historical Society, 1987, p70.
[2] E. Wing, Coroner's Inquest 16 & 23/2/1863, ibid.
[3] F. Butler, ibid.
[4] W. Oliert (also Oleat), Miranda Enquiry, ibid.
[5] Second Lt Hill, ibid.
[6] Evidence, Admiralty Court Martial, ibid.
[7] Lt C.G. Hunt, Miranda Enquiry, ibid.
[8] Fairburn, *The Orpheus Disaster*, pp81-82.
[9] T. Wing, ibid.
[10] Evidence at the Miranda Enquiry, ibid.
[11] Lt Hill to Capt. Jenkins, 8/2/1863, ibid.
[12] Miranda Enquiry, in Fairburn.
[13] Lt Hill to Capt. Jenkins.
[14] T. Wing, *NZ Herald*, 10/7/1880, ibid.
[15] Evidence at the Miranda Enquiry, ibid.
[16] Lt Hill to Capt. Jenkins.
[17] Ibid.

DELAWARE
[1] *Nelson Examiner*, 8/9/1863.
[2] *The Colonist*, 8/9/1863.
[3] H. Skeet, *Nelson Examiner*, 8/9/1863.
[4] W. Morgan, ibid.
[5] Ibid.
[6] *The Colonist*, 8/9/1863.
[7] Ibid.
[8] *Nelson Examiner*, 8/9/1863.
[9] Ibid.
[10] *The Colonist*, 8/9/1863.
[11] *Nelson Examiner*, 8/9/1863.
[12] Coroner's Inquest jury, ibid.
[13] *Nelson Examiner*, 17/11/1863.
[14] J. McAloon, *Nelson: A Regional History*, Cape Catley & Nelson City Council, 1997, p87.

TARARUA
[1] *Melbourne Argus*, 2/5/1881.
[2] The gold was found 3yrs later in a chest after the death of the ship's 2nd steward, R. Hinton.
[3] *Melbourne Argus*, 2/5/1881.
[4] *NZ Herald*, 9 & 12/5/1881.
[5] *NZ Herald*, 13/5/1881.
[6] Ibid.
[7] The order to 'reverse engines' is given in Lindsay, *NZ Herald* 2/5/1881, & in '*Tararua*', J. MacIntosh, 1970 p17. However, the first mate was asleep when the vessel hit the reef & none of those on deck at the time who survived – 4 – mention it in published reports.
[8] *NZ Herald*, 2/5/1881.
[9] *NZ Herald*, 9/5/1881.
[10] *NZ Herald*, 6/5/1881.
[11] Also spelt 'Laurence'.
[12] *NZ Herald*, 2/5/1881.
[13] Also spelt Gilbee, Gellis & Gillbee.
[14] Quoted by W. Doak in *The wreck of the 'Tararua'*, a radio play.
[15] Also spelt Mikallef & Miscellief.
[16] *NZ Herald*, 6/5/1881.
[17] *NZ Herald*, 2 & 16/5/1881.
[18] *NZ Herald*, 6/5/1881.
[19] *NZ Herald*, 9/5/1881.
[20] Ibid.
[21] *NZ Herald*, 2 & 9/5/1881.
[22] *NZ Herald*, 6/5/1881.
[23] W. Doak in *The wreck of the 'Tararua'*.
[24] A.H. Reed, *Farthest South*, Reed, 1953, p39.
[25] *NZ Herald*, 16/5/1881.
[26] Ibid.
[27] *Illustrated NZ Herald*, 16/6/1881.

BEN VENUE
[1] In Shipping Memories, p834.
[2] J.C. Andersen, *Jubilee History of South Canterbury*, Whitcombe & Tombs, 1916, p222.
[3] J.S. Parker, *Timaru Centenary 1868-1968*, C.E. Dawson, 1968, p25.
[4] *Timaru Herald*, 16/1/1882.
[5] Ibid.
[6] Andersen, p227.
[7] Sir H. Brett, *White Wings*, vol.1, pp302-03.
[8] *Timaru Herald*, 15/5/1882.
[9] *Timaru Herald*, 15/6/1882.
[10] *Timaru Herald*, 15/5/1882.
[11] Ibid.
[12] *Timaru Herald*, 23/5 & 15/6/1882.
[13] *Timaru Herald*, 15/5/1882.
[14] *Timaru Herald*, 23/5/1882.
[15] Ibid.
[16] *Timaru Herald*, 17/5/1882.
[17] *Timaru Herald*, 16/5/1882.
[18] *Timaru Herald*, 23/5/1882.
[19] Ibid.
[20] *Timaru Herald*, 15/5/1882.
[21] *Timaru Herald*, 17/5/1882.

ARIADNE
[1] *Otago Daily Times*, 28/3/1901.
[2] G. McLean, *New Zealand Tragedies: Shipwrecks & Maritime Disasters*, Grantham, 1991, p127.
[3] *Otago Daily Times*, 13/4/1901.
[4] S. Willis, *Otago Daily Times*, 1/11/1901.
[5] *Otago Daily Times*, 17/4/1901.
[6] *Otago Daily Times*, 24/1/1902.
[7] *Otago Daily Times*, 22/1/1902.
[8] *Otago Daily Times*, 21/1/1902.
[9] S. Willis, *Otago Daily Times*, 1/11/1901.
[10] P. Attwood, *Otago Daily Times*, 1/11/1901. R. Monigatti says Cape Foulwind in *New Zealand Sensations*, 1962, p24; A.C. Hanlon says 'in the Tasman', *Random Recollections – Notes on a Lifetime at the Bar*, 1939, p154.
[11] *Otago Daily Times*, 1/11/1901.
[12] *Otago Daily Times*, 12/1/1902.
[13] *Otago Daily Times*, 22/1/1902.
[14] Ibid.
[15] K. Catran, *Hanlon A Casebook*, p75.
[16] Ibid.
[17] *Otago Daily Times*, 10/10/1901.
[18] *Otago Daily Times*, 14/10/1901.
[19] *Otago Daily Times*, 12/11/1901.
[20] Hanlon, p156.
[21] *Otago Daily Times*, 20/12/1901.
[22] *Otago Daily Times*, 25/1/1902.
[23] *Otago Daily Times*, 20/12/1901.
[24] *Otago Daily Times*, 25/1/1902.
[25] *Otago Daily Times*, 15/4/1901.
[26] *Otago Daily Times*, 8/1/1902.
[27] Ibid.
[28] *Otago Daily Times*, 23/1/1902.
[29] Ibid.
[30] *Otago Daily Times*, 22/1/1902.
[31] Catran, p75.
[32] *Otago Daily Times*, 25/1/1902.
[33] Hanlon, p157.
[34] *Otago Daily Times*, 25/1/1902.
[35] Ibid.

ELINGAMITE
[1] *NZ Herald*, 17/11/1902.
[2] *Auckland Star*, 14/11/1902.
[3] *NZ Herald*, 14/11/1902.
[4] *Auckland Star*, 15/11/1902.
[5] *NZ Graphic*, 22/11/1902.
[6] A. Robb's memoir.
[7] *Auckland Star*, 13/11/1902.
[8] *NZ Graphic*, 22/11/1902.
[9] A. Robb's memoir.
[10] *Auckland Star*, 13/11/1902.
[11] A. Robb's memoir.
[12] Dr W.H. Goldie, *NZ Herald*, 13/11/1902.
[13] *Auckland Star*, 13/11/1902.
[14] S. Neill, *NZ Graphic*, 22/11/1902.
[15] T. Wetherill, *NZ Herald*, 15/11/1902.
[16] *Auckland Star*, 15/11/1902.
[17] *NZ Herald*, 15/11/1902.

WILTSHIRE
[1] In *NZ Listener*, newspapers of the time & the Newsletter of the Master Mariners – J.H. Musgrove; in NZ Sound Archives & *Sunday Star-Times* – G.H. Musgrove.
[2] J.H. Musgrove, *NZ Listener*, 27/12/1975, pp14-15.
[3] Newsletter New Zealand Co. of Master Mariners (Auckland Branch), 9/1997, p12.
[4] Musgrove, *NZ Listener*.
[5] *Auckland Weekly News*, 8/6/1922, p16.
[6] Musgrove, *NZ Listener*.
[7] Ibid.
[8] Ibid.
[9] *Auckland Weekly News*, 8/6/1922, p16.
[10] Capt. J. Plowman, letter to the Marine Superintendent, USS Co, 12/6/1922.
[11] *Auckland Weekly News*, 8/6/1922, p18.
[12] Musgrove, *NZ Listener*.
[13] *Auckland Weekly News*, 8/6/1922, p16.
[14] Ibid.
[15] Musgrove, *NZ Listener*.
[16] *Auckland Weekly News*, 8/6/1922, p16.
[17] *Auckland Weekly News*, 8/6/1922, p17.
[18] J. Plowman, letter to USS Co.
[19] Musgrove, *NZ Listener*.
[20] Ibid.
[21] *Auckland Weekly News*, 8/6/1922, p19.
[22] USS Co. letter to Plowman, 16/6/1922.

NIAGARA
[1] J. Maynard, *Niagara's Gold*, Kangaroo Press, 1996, p19.
[2] Maynard, p20.
[3] *NZ Herald*, 20/6/1940.
[4] G. McLean, *New Zealand Tragedies, Shipwrecks & Maritime Disasters*, p136.
[5] Maynard, p20.
[6] *NZ Herald*, 20/6/1940.
[7] Ibid.
[8] Ibid.
[9] Maynard, pp43-44.
[10] Ibid, p48.
[11] Ibid, p53.
[12] Ibid, p104.
[13] Ibid, p120.
[14] Ibid, p132.

TURAKINA
[1] K. Weyher, Letter to NZ Shipping Co., 1962.
[2] K. Weyher & H.J. Ehrlich, *The Black Raider*, Elek Books, 1955, p91.
[3] Weyher, p92.
[4] Ibid, p92.
[5] S.D. Waters, *Ordeal by Sea, The New Zealand Shipping Company in the Second World War, 1939-1945*, NZ Shipping Co., 1949, pp17-18.
[6] Ibid, p23.
[7] Ibid, p20.
[8] Ibid.
[9] Ibid, pp20-21.
[10] Weyher, p93.
[11] Ibid, pp94-95.
[12] Ibid, p95.
[13] Peter Fraser, PM, telegram sent to Mrs Laird, Scotland, 29/8/1940.
[14] *NZ Herald*, 24/8/1944.
[15] *NZ Herald*, 28/1/1941.
[16] *NZ Herald*, 30/1/1941.
[17] *NZ Herald*, 27/8/1941.
[18] *The Dominion*, 26/1/1941.
[19] Waters, *Ordeal by Sea*, p24.
[20] S.D. Waters, *Royal New Zealand Navy*, Dept of Internal Affairs, 1956, p128.

HOLMGLEN
[1] P.W. Spinetto, "When I was on Raoul!" – The Raoul Island Expedition, 1957.
[2] P.A.T. Gordon, former chief officer on the *Holmglen*, at the Court of Inquiry, 1960.
[3] NZPA, 25/11/1959.
[4] NZPA, *Timaru Herald*, 11/1959.
[5] M. Geddes, interview, Greenstone 1999.
[6] Official log, *Holmburn*, 5/10/1959 – 8/4/1960, National Archives.
[7] B. Jenkins, interview, Greenstone 1999.
[8] A. Grieve, interview, Greenstone 1999.
[9] NZPA 25/11/1959.
[10] R. Donald, interview, Greenstone 1999.
[11] Official log, *Holmburn*.
[12] Donald, MV *Nella*'s Report on *Holmglen*.
[13] Donald, interview, Greenstone 1999.
[14] *Timaru Herald*.
[15] Ibid.
[16] NZPA, coroner's inquest, 1959.
[17] M. Geddes, interview, Greenstone 1999.
[18] K. McCallum, interview, Greenstone 1999.
[19] A. Grieve, interview, Greenstone 1999.
[20] B. Jenkins, interview, Greenstone 1999.
[21] D.W. Virtue, Court of Inquiry.